FROM CAROL BROOKS
4-19-17

# An Extraordinary

# Ordinary Life

BY

## DEAN O. WEBB

Boynton Beach, Florida

Cover Design & Copy Editing by Judy Walters

Dean O. Webb has made every effort to trace the ownership of any scripture, poems and quotes. In the event of any questions arising from the use of same, we regret any error and will be pleased to make the necessary corrections in future editions of this book.

**An Extraordinary Ordinary Life**
**ISBN-10# 1542613299**
**ISBN-13# 9781542613293**
Copyright © 2016 by Dean O. Webb

For more information, write:

Dean O. Webb
c/o Faith Farm Ministries
9538 US Highway 441
Boynton Beach, FL  33472

# TABLE OF CONTENTS

# DEDICATION

I dedicate this book to the memory of my Father, whose life established in me the concept of faith in God and the legacy of trusting God in all things ... to trust that God has plans for you that are for your ultimate good, no matter how bleak a situation is at the time. God knows our future and how our story ends ... we do not. We just have to trust Him, pray in faith, and ask with pure motives.

Like most people, I have had some bad things happen to me in my life. In addition, I have had many extraordinary things happen, and some incredible answers to prayer. Come take this life journey with this ordinary boy from Oklahoma, who lived through some extraordinary life experiences.

Dean O. Webb

# ACKNOWLEDGEMENTS

There are so many people involved in the writing of a book such as this. Most of the credit must go to Judy Walters, who provided much needed suggestions on all facets of the book and its design. She researched publishing and provided the framework from publishing specs to copy editing. She formatted and facilitated the publishing of the pages and designed the book's cover. Thanks, Judy.

Thank you to my daughter, Catherine Webb Williams, for the creative title for the book, and heartfelt thanks is due to Amy Keefe for her time and expertise in proofreading the book.

Finally, I express a very loving thank you to my wife, Cindy, for her unconditional, selfless support by graciously allowing me to be absent from our Saturdays together for a couple of years in order for me to work on this project. Cindy always puts others before herself and is the kindest soul I've ever known.

For my children, this has been a work of love by me, who strongly desires that the legacy of the faith of Catherine and Christine's grandfather be known, and also to preserve many of the life events of their father to his children. I can only hope that each reader also finds these experiences interesting.

Dean O. Webb

# MY LIFE PURPOSE

To provide an opportunity for you
to experience the courage
to demonstrate your faith in God
so that you will experience His power.

# MY LIFE VERSE

*Give and it shall be given to you: good measure, pressed down, and shaken together, and running over, shall men give into your bosom. For with the same measure that ye mete withal it shall be measured to you again.* Luke 6:38 KJV

# PREFACE

I never wanted an ordinary life. I wanted excitement. I wanted to travel the world and live life's experiences to the fullest ... all of it. Growing up in Oklahoma, I was deathly afraid of being trapped into living an ordinary, dull life ... passing through this one span of time, *my life,* without experiencing all the various things life had to offer. My father was so strict that I knew those experiences would have to come when I was older and away from the home. Little did I expect that my life's roller coaster of ups-and-downs would start when I was only age 12! On Thanksgiving morning in 1953, my father died in an automobile accident, and my life's rollercoaster of experiences began. That first extraordinary experience was bad. Later on, others were good. Actually, I have had a lifetime mixed with both good and bad experiences.

I remember when I was first stricken by seeing the old poster of a navy sailor pointing out toward the viewer saying, "Join the Navy and See the World." *"Yes,"* I thought, *"I want that."* I eventually joined the Navy and got to see 50 countries. (Good) I wanted to be a millionaire by age 40, and was a *multi*-millionaire by age 40. (Good); but, then I lost it all ... (which was bad.) I wanted to build a large home, and I built an 11,000 sq. ft. home on 32 acres in Atlanta. (Good) Then I lost it in a bank auction (bad.) I wanted to hold an elected office; go to a Presidential inaugural ball in Washington, D.C.; be on radio and TV; experience miracles from God; witness miracles of others in testimonials; be one of the first members of my family to graduate from college; experience a miraculous healing; all of those things! I did experience all of those things, which ended up good. I even came close to being shot out of the sky in Vietnam. I lived without harm. That was good.

When I think of all the ups-and-downs of life, especially the extremes, I often wonder how people who lack a close connection to God are able to deal with them. One minute, I am dealing with the pride that creeps in with financial success; then dealing with the devastation of financial ruin; loss of a wife you love; a near-death experience in Vietnam; or the perspective of a miraculous answer to prayer. To trust God in all the extraordinary ups-and-downs of life's experiences is the anchor of my life. I know He is in control, and He knows what He is doing.

Many times, I have been in a conversation in a group of people about events of life, and I would chime in on an experience that I had related to that particular subject being discussed. Invariably, someone at the table would say, "You should write that down … you need to write a book." After numerous occasions like this, I began to be aware that I was fortunate to have a huge variety of experiences unique to the average person's life that not everyone had experienced. Not everyone had made and lost millions. Not everyone had lost a loving spouse. Not everyone was almost shot down in Vietnam. Not everyone had experienced a miraculous healing. Not everyone had flipped a coin with an IRS agent to determine what taxes they owed. Not everyone had seen his or her Dad do incredible things of faith and logic. Not everyone has had a State Legislature name a day after his wife when she died. Not everyone has trusted God for answers to prayer that took relentless years of prayer to bring about the answer... or, to see a miraculous answer to a Dad's prayer in a matter of minutes. Not everyone has worked 5-6 jobs a day while in college, and to graduate college debt free, without receiving grants or scholarships and no loans to pay back. Not everyone has awakened to the scratching sound of giant roaches crawling all over the walls and floors in a hotel room in a foreign land. Not everyone has been brought into a non-profit organization by a Board of Directors through a headhunter to turn around an organization that was losing 2.6 million a year and being a part of its rescue.

There are just a lot of extraordinary events outside of the average person's norm that I wanted to preserve for my family and others who might be interested. This is my version of "An Extraordinary Ordinary Life."


Dean O. Webb

# OLD NEWSPAPER ARTICLES FROM 1949

Upper Left is the children's orphanage supported by the Beams of Light Tabernacle Church, pastored by my Dad, Rev. O. W. Webb, a renowned radio minister. Upper right is the parsonage, which also housed the boys.

Rev. Webb, at the extreme left, poses with his children in the orphanage.

# DINNER at the ORPHANAGE

*"If ye abide in me, and my words abide in you, ye shall ask
what ye will, and it shall be done unto you."* John 15:7

I was only nine, and my father was huddled in the kitchen with the orphanage director and the other women of the kitchen staff. I could overhear them telling my father that they had absolutely no food in the house to cook for supper. It was 5:30 pm; time to eat dinner. Normally, the kitchen staff would have finished cooking the evening meal long before now, and the children were seated for dinner. The children were expecting to eat. Before now, dinner was always on time.

I remember hearing one of the cooks crying, while exclaiming that she just could not handle telling the children they were not going to eat that night. While waiting for dinner call, they all played out in the yard on swing sets and teeter-totters, playing tag and just having fun. The children were completely unaware of the no-food situation in the orphanage kitchen. My father said, "We'll just call the children in and pray for dinner to come." Everyone knew my Dad was a pastor who was a pillar of faith in God, but this just might be going a little too far. Nevertheless, I remember my father telling the staff to call all the little children in from the yard to take their seats in the dining room.

The orphanage was in a mansion on 48 acres that had once been the estate of an owner of a major oil company. The lovely dining room, elegantly attired in silk curtains and flocked wallpaper, must have held some beautiful, formal dinners in times past. Previously, the huge dining room held a table for 12 with a spacious amount of room behind the chairs for servants to serve everyone. There was plenty of room for them to move around

17

easily behind all the seated guests. That dining set was removed. Two long, parallel tables with folding chairs lined up on both sides of each row of tables replaced the huge dining room furnishings. The orphanage was home to about 24 children, ages 3 to 12. They took their seats on either side of the multiple long tables and bowed their heads, while my father cried out to God with an impassioned plea for His provision and thanked Him for the food that they were about to receive.

Upon the completion of his prayer, he told the children to go back out and play, and they would be called in again when the food was prepared ... that it was not ready just yet. Looking very disappointed, they filed back out the door to resume playing in the yard. I overheard one of the older girl's remarks that she could not figure out what was for dinner that night, since she could not smell anything cooking.

You can probably imagine the backlash from the staff against my father ... toned down a bit, of course. After all, he was their boss ... their employer. They had seen my father trust God for the impossible before, but nothing this close to home ... missing dinner for the children. There were remarks like, "not being honest" with the children; how this was going to "destroy their faith in God." What was my father going to do now? I overheard one staff member say that my father's strong faith had finally allowed him to "paint himself into a corner."

While my father was defending God and his belief in God and miracles, a miracle occurred. Right in the midst of all this loud talking, a huge delivery truck pulled up. The truck was under the front portico on the opposite side of the back yard where the children were playing. The driver jumped out to verify that he was at the Beams of Light Children's Home.   Upon receiving that assurance, he told of a man who had heard my Dad's daily radio broadcast speaking about the lives of young, rescued children. The broadcast motivated the man to provide a truckload of food to the orphanage. You can imagine the clapping of hands, the overwhelming jubilation and the shouting of "Praise the Lord" when boxes and boxes of canned goods, meats, sauces, and gallons of olives, pickles and other condiments were unloaded. Two women immediately began cooking up hot dishes, even while others were unloading the truck.

That meal was the happiest meal of my life. I do not even remember what the food was. I only remember that my Dad had not embarrassed himself. Truthfully, I was grateful he did not embarrass me by sticking his neck out to trust and believe God, again.  That was simply the way my father lived. God always came through on time, though not often early.

I thought back to a time I was riding in the car with my father when he drove into this gated, 48-acre estate ... the orphanage. The huge, heavily landscaped, ornate home had tall, ornate, wrought-iron gates and fencing. It had a driveway under porticos on each side of the home, ornate fountains with fish ponds, huge rooms, green marble showers with multiple shower heads, and a 4-car detached garage with apartments above that were all elegantly landscaped. My Dad got out of the car and knocked on the door of this oilman's home. He told the woman who answered the door that God had told him to buy this home for an orphanage. I could tell by the woman's voice and body language that the response was not exactly cordial. He returned to the car and exclaimed, *in an almost surprised tone of voice*, that the owners did not share his vision for the home to be an orphanage.  I heard my Dad exclaim that he knew he had, "heard from God." By now, I knew not to question my father.

Some months later, my Dad received a call. The owners were divorcing and they asked my father if he was still interested in purchasing the estate. That is how the orphanage in Tulsa started ... by faith, and it continued to operate by faith. He said, "Yes," and bought it for cents on the dollar to settle the divorce conflict.

When I was going through some tough, trying times later in my adult life, the *tape* that always played in my head from my father's life was that ANYTHING was possible if you only believed. My father modeled faith before me daily. I never knew what it was like for God NOT to come through. I learned not to argue with my Dad when he stood on John 15:7. After all, He did say, *"If ye abide in me, and my words abide in you, ye shall ask what ye will, and it shall be done unto you."* John 15:7. My father made that verse come alive. He made it real to me. He was living proof that anything was possible if you met the condition of *abiding in Him*. My father was a man of faith in God, and I am fortunate to have my heritage through him. This story depicts one of the most memorable, cherished and extraordinary experiences of my life.

# CAN YOU SAY "STRICT"?

*"Train up a child in the way he should go: and when he is old,
he will not depart from it."* Proverbs 22:6

To say that my Pentecostal preacher-pastor father was strict is a gross understatement, especially by modern standards, for sure. While growing up, we were not allowed to participate in *mixed bathing*. In other words, boys and girls in swimsuits could not go swimming in the same pool or lake at the same time. At our annual camp meeting, for example, we had to divide the afternoon hours. The girls had to be out of the lake swim area by the time the boys arrived for their turn to swim.

We could not have a deck of cards in the house. We could have children's card games like Old Maid or Crazy Eights, for example, but not a regular deck of cards that one would use for poker, casinos or gambling.

We could not see or play with dice. In fact, when we got our first Monopoly game at Christmas, my Dad quickly confiscated the dice out of the game. He gave me a stiff, white piece of cardboard that was in one of his laundered shirts and had me draw a circle on it, divide the circle into 12 pie-shaped wedges from the center of the circle, and number the wedges "1" through "12". We cut a cardboard piece into an "arrow" shape and stuck a straight pin through the center of the circle drawn on the cardboard. That was our *spinner,* and we would flick it with our fingernails to substitute for the numbers "one though 12" we might have rolled with the dice. However inconvenient or ridiculous it seemed, it worked, and we got by.

As far as smoking, drinking, movies or dancing ... forget it!

I could not believe that we were not allowed to go to the movies. Based upon the movie content back in the 40's and 50's, I am not exactly sure what I could have seen that would have corrupted me. A couple of years after my father died when I was age 14, my older sister, Ann, finally got my mother to agree to let Ann take me to the movies. The movie was *The Robe.* Although parts of the story of Christ's robe was probably inaccurate and created to make for a good story, it was still very moving. I was very touched. I have been hooked on going to movies ever since. That love for going to the theater extends to Broadway musicals. I now love live theater. I have been to dozens of Broadway plays in New York. I do not get near New York City without making a Broadway play a must while there. When my daughter wanted to see a play for her birthday, I took my daughter to New York to see *Les Misérables.* I was so smitten that when we returned to Atlanta, I took my wife and turned right around, and flew back up to New York to see *Les Misérables* with her, too. It is still my favorite musical today.

I am not sure what was in my Dad's mind as to why my Dad did not want me to go to theaters. Maybe he thought my innocent eyes would see something that would scar me. Perhaps he sensed that I would become obsessive compulsive about movies, stories, plays, and musicals. In any event, maybe he was right. My first time did *hook* me; but cards, dice, swimming ... not so much. I do love to be near the water (pool, ocean, beach, river), but just *to look* at it, not necessarily to go *in* it. I just love the atmosphere that always accompanies a water view, especially the ocean and the sound of waves breaking on the shore.

I lived through the extraordinary rigors of absurd strictness, and came out undamaged. I can say I did not get into any trouble growing up. I mean … who could, with all of those rules?

Growing up, I hated all the strict rules and was unhappy and rebellious against them. Now that I am grown, I see all the problems people deal with because their parents were less strict and controlling. I can now say that I am glad my father was extraordinarily strict. In my life, I have not had to deal with overuse of drugs, alcohol, unwanted pregnancies, or gambling addictions because of my father's strict controls on my life. As Proverbs 22:6 says, *"Train up a child in the way he should go: and when he is old he will not depart from it."*

Pictured from left to right in this early family photo are my younger brother, Jerry; my father; my younger sister, Ruth; my mother; me; my older sister, Ann.

# WATERMELON BEFORE CHURCH

*"Honor thy father and thy mother."* Exodus 20:12

Oh no, I just could not hold it any longer. I was peeing in my pants in church. I sat at the right end of the front row, center wooden pew. Evidently, this was "high ground." I know, because the stream was running down the pew away from me to my left down the entire center pew. I just could not hold it in, and it was a full bladder, for sure.

We all had watermelon before we left for church on Sunday night, and it had just culminated in a torrent of urine. Earlier, I had signaled my Dad (the Pastor) on the platform that I had to "go." He snapped his fingers and motioned for me to sit still. I had signaled again, and again the "no!" I even mouthed the words, "I have to go to the bathroom." He saw me, but still said no. In all fairness to my father, I was always pushing the envelope of rules. I suppose he figured I was just trying to weasel my way out of church again. I felt like we practically "lived" in church.

My dilemma was that if I continued to sit still, I was going to go to the bathroom in my pants. If I disobeyed and went up the aisle anyway, he would have given me a whipping for disobedience when we got home. I seriously considered the consequence of the whipping in private, being less painful than the agony of embarrassment in public, but stayed put. In fact, this had gone on so long that I knew I was past the point of no return. I could no longer "keep it in" even if I had chosen to disobey. By now, I knew that if I got up and walked briskly down the long aisle to the back of the church, I would not have made it. I would have soiled myself right in the middle of the aisle, while walking to the rear of the

25

church. So here I was, going to the bathroom anyway, on the front pew of the center row of the church.

Now, if everyone was sitting in their seats, everyone might have exited out the back of the church at the end of the service, and no one would have ever known. I could have stayed seated and just waited until they all left before I stood up to leave. However, my Dad delivered such a powerful message, and the invitation to *get right with God* motivated people to pour down the aisles to the altar to pray. There were so many people responding that the altars in front were full on both sides. Because the altars were full, they turned and knelt at the center front pew to pray ... the pew where I was sitting.

Can you see it? People lined up, shoulder to shoulder, across the center front pew, kneeling over with their elbows resting on the front pew while praying. Opening their eyes momentarily in their prayer, sensing or smelling something strange, those kneeling in prayer, beginning with those closest to me, began to lift their heads in perfect sequence down the row in 4-5 second intervals, saying "Oh no," or "Oh my God," or "What are you doing?" Like the famous Rockettes, choreographed by the famous Radio City Music Hall, their heads rose one-by-one going from those closest to me to those away from me down the whole row in perfect order. Each one in sequence was becoming acutely aware that their tears were falling on my pee, which was running down the length of the back of the pew. Honestly, the Rockettes' well-choreographed, leg kicking sequence had nothing on this head-bobbing sequence. One by one in perfect sequence, each head popped up and looked at me. They could see the source of the flow ... me ... the little kid at the other end of the church pew. The pastor's son had done it again. It was at that moment that I felt I should have risked the humiliation of the whipping at home, rather than the humiliation in public. I learned, however, that you obey your parents no matter what, and I survived.

Parents, it is not fair to feed your children watermelon right before church. No one wins on that one, except that I can honestly say I honored my father in obedience to him. It resulted in an extraordinary experience … actually, one that I wish I could forget.

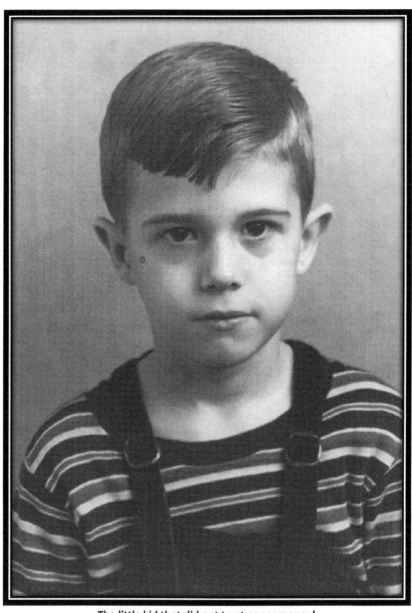

The little kid that did not trust paper money!

# NO PAPER MONEY

My father drove up into the front yard one afternoon and saw that it was full of potholes. It appeared the holes were dug randomly throughout the entire front yard, like a pot-holed war-zone. In fact, it appeared that the yard was overtaken by a plague of gophers. To explain the reason for this, I have to go back several years.

Ever since I can remember, I never understood why we had paper money. It seemed so unwise. I was always afraid it could burn up, rot, mildew or be destroyed some other way. I felt that metal was more durable and safe. Therefore, I always converted my paper money earnings from mowing neighbors' lawns and doing other odd jobs into silver … silver dollars or half dollars. *There! Now that feels safe and more permanent.*

When I finally filled my metal box with silver coins I had saved, I decided I needed even more safety. Inspired by stories of pirates in books, I decided to bury my treasure. I took the box, grabbed a pencil and paper, my cub-scout compass, a shovel, and went to the front yard of our house. We were on 2 acres so I had lots of room to work with for my burial location. The anchor point of my "plan" was that I needed to start from a permanent point … one that could not be moved or changed in any way. I knew the starting point could not be a tree. A tree might die and then be cut down. I decided that the water spigot sticking out of the home's front stacked, stone wall was very permanent; at least as permanent as the house.

I backed up to the water spigot with my heels firmly placed against the base of the wall, and headed due South by the compass, carefully counting the steps. I was so careful to place the heel of one shoe on each next step against the toe of my other shoe from the last step, so that the number of steps would be precise. At a certain point, I stopped, made a record of the step count total, turned a perfect 90-degree right turn by the compass, and headed due west. Again, I was careful to be as precise on the heel-to-toe steps as in the last direction.

I drew both compass directions and number of steps on my "Treasure Map." I placed a stone on the destination spot, and then ran back to the house spigot with my map and compass. I carefully replicated my first compass direction and number of steps, then the same on the second leg of steps. I needed to make sure there was no error, so I could find the spot again sometime in the future. This second time, I verified that it was the exact same spot as the first time. Happy with my precision, I dug a hole and buried my silver "treasure." I was eight years old.

The summer I turned 12, I had an urge to dig up my treasure. I found my carefully guarded old secret "treasure map," grabbed a shovel, compass, backed up to the spigot, sighted the compass direction, and followed the precise heel-to-toe steps in both directions as I had done when I created the treasure burial spot location. Upon arriving at the measured spot, I began to dig at the depth I remembered (I had not recorded the depth,) and the treasure was not there. Maybe I buried it deeper than I remembered. I kept digging; still no treasure! Thinking I might be off a bit, I widened the hole and deepened the hole. Still, there was no metal box! Allowing for being off a bit, I dug another hole to one side and then another side; then past the assumed spot; then

30

shortened the spot for the next hole. Beginning to panic, I began to think that I might have recorded the wrong digit … maybe it was 20 steps … not 30 … another hole! I moved 10 feet in all four compass directions. Still, I found no treasure!

That was about the time my father drove up. I had hoped to dig my anticipated one hole, and refill the hole quickly before he came home. I had so little time between school dismissal and dinnertime. Instead, the front yard was full of holes, flanked by mounds of dirt by them. I could see the distressed, questioning look on my father's face. He was visibly upset. With hands on both hips, he asked, "What do you think you're doing?"

I told him in detail exactly what I had done when I was eight, and I showed him my map with all the directions and number of steps I had recorded for each direction. He thought for a moment, then laughed, and headed into the house. He went back to my bedroom I shared with my younger brother, Jerry. I was eight when I paced off my steps. My brother was now seven, and I guess my Dad figured that was close enough. He took my dress shoe, and one of my brother's dress shoes, and measured the difference between my 12-year-old shoe and my brother's seven-year-old shoe. He then multiplied the difference by the number of original paces I made in each direction to get the shortened distance in feet and inches I was off in each direction.

We then went back outside to the spigot and I carefully followed the first compass direction's heel-to-toe pace. My father then subtracted back the distance my current foot size measured more than my brother's smaller size, times the number of steps, to estimate where I would have been years ago. I backed up to that spot, then turned 90-degrees and paced off the precise heel-to-toe

31

measurements in the second direction. My father then again subtracted and measured back the difference my 12-year-old shoe was from my brother's shoe for the number of paces. At that spot, my father said, "Dig here." We were close enough. With a slightly wider hole than originally dug and a much shallower hole than I remembered as a boy of eight, I heard the sound of shovel against metal. There it was ... my buried "Treasure."

Of course, I spent the balance of daylight after dinner refilling holes and packing the dirt down into them. I did not care because I had found my "treasure." All the while, I thought, "How smart is my Dad?" What an extraordinary experience!

I have never forgotten that event. It was just one more way I was proud of my father. Proverbs 17:6 is true ... *"The glories of children are their fathers."*

# FIRE RESCUE

*"Then they cry unto the Lord in their trouble,*
*and He saveth them out of their distress."* Psalms 107:19

I was so happy to be riding with my dad to one of his speaking engagements. He was looking very sharp in a three-piece suit with a vest and tie, and ready to step into the pulpit upon arrival. I recall it being very dark as we were slowly going around the mountainous road at night. The steep mountain wall was on our left, and a huge drop-off was on the right ... the side I was riding on. If it had not been so dark, I might have been even more scared if I could see how far down the drop-off was.

We were making a long, slow turn on the curve to the left, and I saw a glow in the night up ahead around the bend. It was a yellow, flickering, light that got brighter as we progressed around the slow left turn. Suddenly, in the black of the night, we rounded the turn and the light was blindingly bright. It was a huge fire. A car coming the opposite way had stopped in the other lane, up against the cliff. The car was engulfed in flames. In the illumination of the fire, we could see a man trapped in the front driver's seat screaming for help.

My Dad stopped, immediately ran in front of our car, and removed his suit coat as he was crossing the road. He used his coat to shield his face, then to insulate his hand against the heat of the door handle, and jerked the door open and pulled the man out of the burning car and onto the pavement. The man's clothes were in flames, and my Dad was using his suit coat to beat out the flames and to smother the final flames until there was none.

He ran back to our car and grabbed his Bible from the front seat, and went running back to the lifeless man on the ground. In the glow of the fire, he knelt down in the road, read scriptures and prayed with the man. In case this were that man's final time on earth, since he was still conscious, my dad was going to make sure he was right with God.

I never did know the outcome of that event ... whether the man died or not. As other cars arrived, my Dad was barking orders…. He had some attend to the victim… he asked some to go for help to the nearest town. In the early 1950's, there were no cell phones, so help had to be sought by driving to a town to access a phone booth, or if lucky, find a phone booth on the way to speed up the process of seeking medical help. I remember continuing on to arrive late at the church. My Dad stood in the pulpit to speak without his suit coat, which remained with the victim.

About 45 years later, I attended a movie called, The Apostle, starring Robert Duvall. In the movie, the preacher played by Duvall was nothing of the good character of my father. However, in that movie, Duvall encountered a multiple car accident. Wrecked cars were scattered over the highway with police directing traffic around the wreckages. Spotting a car that had gone over the embankment, Duvall grabs his Bible off the front seat of his car and navigates over the slight hill down to the wrecked car. The husband, who was driving, and his wife appeared to be dead. However, when Duvall detects some life in the driver's eyes, he lays his Bible on top of the car, leans into the car, and begins to minister to the man to accept Jesus into his heart before he dies. The flashback of my father in the similar situation was so powerful and emotional that I got up and left the theatre. I never finished the movie because it was an emotional, powerful scene etched in my mind from a real life memory. The flashback of that extraordinary experience was just too powerful to continue. That experience placed an indelible impression on my mind as a child, even more than I realized.

In retrospect, I think about my father and all the good he did. He was a kind servant of mankind. He never thought twice about the risk of jumping in to help someone in trouble … not just physically, but spiritually. I only have proud thoughts of my father. What a heritage he left me. When I think of that man trapped in his car on fire, I have an indelible imprint in my mind of a real life situational example of Psalms 107:19, which says, *"Then they cry unto the Lord in their troubles, and He saveth   them out of their distress."* God used my father to pull that man out of the flames.

# FAITH for ULCERS

*"For as the body without the spirit is dead,
so faith without works is dead also."* James 2:26

At 10 years old, I could not eat anything; especially something fun ... Pizza, steak, popcorn, chili ... nothing good; nothing spicy. A slice of toast floating in a bowl of heated milk was my usual meal. If I even ate vegetables, my stomach would hurt. If I ate meat, for example, I would spit up blood for days. If I took a drink of a carbonated soda, like Coke or Pepsi, my stomach would burn and pain for days. Stomach ulcers are not fun.

I had always been a skinny, puny kid. I was born so sick that I was not healthy enough to go home from the hospital until I was 8-weeks old. I had Undulant Fever and Whooping Cough (Pertussis) as a newborn infant ... *but stomach ulcers ... at 10 years old?* As a sophomore in high school, I was 6- ft. 2-inches tall but weighed only 118 pounds. (I have since rectified that low weight problem). I was born the proverbial weakling.

I had been through the Springer Clinic in Tulsa, Oklahoma numerous times for my ulcers. I never want to stand in front of an x-ray fluoroscope and drink a chalky barium milkshake again. There seemed to be no relief or cure, and the whole family was exhausted from my never-ending, medical ailments.

One Saturday, unexpectedly, my father came home from his church office, put me in the car and said, "We're going back to the Church." An evangelist from Topeka, Kansas, was there to do a weeklong series of special nightly services the following week. It was said that Clem Foster had the God-given "gift of healing." When he laid hands on people and prayed for their healing, miracles occurred ... often. My father said he was going to have him lay hands on me and pray for my healing from the ulcers. *"That's great! I'll be able to eat again,"* I thought.

At the church, Clem Foster took out a small vial of olive oil, anointed my head by touching the oil to my head, laid both hands on me and prayed a very powerful prayer for my healing. I felt nothing. My father thanked him and told him to get rest before the next night's service. (The church had a small apartment in the basement for guest speakers to stay.) After thanking him again, we got in the car to leave.

My father turned left out of the church parking, toward town, not back toward home. I asked where we were going, and my father said, "To the Tulsa Chili Bowl restaurant for chili and a Pepsi." I began to cry. I reminded my Dad that anything with meat, beans, or anything with spices in it would upset my stomach and make me sick for days. Anything carbonated, like a Pepsi, would cause me to cough up blood and keep me from sleeping for days.

My father said that he had faith that I was healed. He said that faith without works is dead and we needed to eat the worst thing I could eat that bothered me, in faith, to show I was healed. For my father, the "work of faith" as evidence that he believed I was healed, was to eat chili. He said, "You will not be bothered by the food." Not convinced, I continued to protest and cry.

I could not stop crying. I refused to eat after the food came and was served. Quietly, but firmly, my father insisted (*demanded*) that I eat the chili. When I refused again, my father quietly, lovingly, but firmly, took me outside the restaurant and spanked me. After allowing me to stop crying and dry my eyes, we then went back inside. I still refused to eat, so out again for another

38

whipping. After multiple whippings and the embarrassing feelings and humiliation from all the eyes in the restaurant on me, I figured it would be better to be in pain alone for days, coughing up blood, losing sleep, and suffering in private silence, than to endure my father's relentless determination to make me eat. The whole ordeal was becoming such an embarrassing public spectacle.

Therefore, I ate the chili and drank the Pepsi. I waited for the internal stomach war to begin. Nothing happened. I ate more and more … still nothing. After finishing the whole bowl of chili and the Pepsi, it became obviously and blatantly clear, my father was right. I was healed instantly.

To this day, my stomach is never upset by anything I eat. Between the U.S. Navy, personal vacations and travel, I have been in over 50 countries. I have eaten some pretty awful, foreign, spicy food, and I never got sick. As a Navy aircraft crewmember, I have eaten the same thing the whole crew ate in other countries, and I did not get sick, even when they all did. I was healed miraculously. My father was right. At the time, the scene in the Tulsa Chili Bowl was horrible. However, the aftermath of healing has been wonderful. I have the strongest stomach I know of … and, I was completely healed! When God heals, He really does it up royally and permanently. I do believe the Word when it says God honors our faith … at least He honored my father's faith for me.

The few times I have told this story, I have had people make remarks like, "Your father was cruel to put you through that," or some similar comment. I can honestly say that I never, not even for a split second, thought anything like that. I knew my father was a man of faith who accomplished great things. I knew he loved me dearly, and I knew he had only the best desires for my life. I knew my father would have never pushed that envelope unless he was convinced, in his spirit, that God had miraculously touched and healed my body.

I am glad my father got sick and tired of seeing me sick and tired, and then took positive, proactive steps to get me better, finally. Everyone should be so fortunate to have a father that was an example of the walk of faith we all talk about, but rarely get to see. Without him, I would have never had my extraordinary healing experience. As James 2:26 says, *"Faith without works is dead faith."*

I believe than anyone reading this would have to conclude that this truly was an extraordinary experience. It transformed my life permanently.

# DREAMS COME TRUE

*"And your young men shall see visions,*
*and your old men shall dream dreams."* Acts 2:17

There was ice everywhere ... not snow, but ice. It was so typical of Atlanta's one ice storm night per year. Not realizing it was coated in clear ice, I stepped off the curb, my feet went backwards, and I flipped forward immediately down on my head on the icy pavement. I was conscious, because I was aware there was blood oozing onto the ice from my forehead. It was not serious, but I was stunned and a little groggy. That is not the interesting part.

The interesting part was that I had been dreaming every night that I fell and hit my head. In one dream, I hit my head while playing football with my brother and friends. In another, I tripped over something and hit my head. In another dream, I fell down a flight of stairs in my home, sliding headfirst the whole length of the stairs from the second story to the first floor, hitting my head into the wall at the base of the stairs. I suspect these were numerous dream "warnings" that I did not heed or even think about. At least I did not think about it enough for me to consider it a premonition to be careful on the icy curb that morning.

After that, I began to be more aware of my dreams as being a warning, foretelling, or a premonition of events to come. However, at that time, it appeared to be a one-time event. My dreams became more meaningful in the future.

# DREAMS

*"Then thou scarest me with dreams,
and terrifies me thru visions."* Job 7:14

"Oh my God, my father's dead," I said as I suddenly sat upright in my bed from a deep sleep. I had just dreamed that the plane he was piloting crashed, and he had not survived.

My mother heard me cry out and ran into my bedroom to comfort me. She assured me that my father was in his bed and safely asleep. It took a while, but my heart finally stopped pounding hard, and I eventually dropped off into sleep again.

The next night was the same. I dreamed that my father died. My father was found dead. Only this time, he had been poisoned on a mission trip. Again, my mother assured me that my father was just fine and asleep in the next room.

The next night … again, the same … my father was dead. He had gone into a bad area of town to help some homeless people, and he was shot to death. I bolted upright in bed, heart pounding again. Again, the reassurance came from my mom that my dad was in bed and safely asleep.

This went on for almost a month in November 1953. It was becoming difficult to fall asleep for fear of another nightmare about my father's death. I dreamed of his death in about every way possible; his plane crashed, a train crash, shooting, stabbing, poisoning and drowning. I dreamed of him dying in just about every way … except an auto accident.

That same month, on Thanksgiving morning in 1953, we were all getting ready to go to church. The new, enlarged sanctuary and classrooms in my father's church were to be dedicated. In attendance were ministers from the different churches in various states that were affiliated with my father's church in Tulsa. The annual Thanksgiving Convention was to last from Thanksgiving morning on Thursday through the following Sunday morning service. Everyone had great anticipation of this annual event. Then the sedan brought several pastors to our home, who notified my mother that my father had been killed in an auto accident.

The shocking news left me numb. Initially, it felt just like another one of my vivid dreams, only a car accident this time. When I look back, it is as if God knew how badly I was going to take the news of my father's death and had spent a month conditioning me for it emotionally through my dreams. It did not alleviate a shock or pain, but acertain numbness was there to cushion the initial shock of the news. Because of my dreams night after night, I felt like I had lived through many "deaths." Now, I can be grateful for that dreamtime conditioning, although I was not grateful at the time. Looking back, I actually feel that God was being merciful, allowing the extraordinary repetition of my dreams to condition me emotionally for this shock. At barely age 12, I was suddenly without a father, and I was the "man" of the house. I felt so alone!

# THANKSGIVING MORNING, 1953

*"For to me to live is Christ, and to die is gain."* Philippians 1:21
*(On my father's gravestone)*

The black sedan pulled up in front of the house on Thanksgiving morning, and several preachers from the various churches associated with my father's church in Tulsa got out of the car. Seeing so many ministers from the various churches from out of town and out of state dropping by seemed a little unusual since my father was not home. As in other years, the ministers were all in town for the Annual Thanksgiving Minister's Convention that would run from Thursday through Sunday. My father was not home because he left immediately after his live radio broadcast from his Pastor's office in his church to drive to Bristow, Oklahoma, to pray for his secretary's mother who was very ill. Dad was very tired but drove to pray for her anyway. He was trying to accomplish the trip and get back in time for the morning service at Church. He had slept little for the previous three nights when making the many preparations for the Thanksgiving convention and celebration. Knowing how tired he was, he probably should not have gone, but my Dad was not one to omit any part of life if it could fit into the schedule.

It was to be a big celebration and dedication of the new, larger sanctuary, the fellowship hall and classroom addition at my dad's church with all the related churches from multiple cities and states to be in representation. However, the somber expression on the entire group of faces as they exited the sedan and walked up the front walkway was a little scary.

I could not overhear what they were telling my mother after they asked her to be seated, but her cries out let me know instantly

45

that she was in emotional pain. Then one of the ministers came over to me to tell me that my father had been killed in an auto accident. He was driving to Bristow, Oklahoma, about 40 miles from Tulsa, in hopes he could get back before the service started. He went to Bristow to pray for his secretary's mother, who was seriously ill. They told us my father fell asleep at the wheel, hit a bridge abutment at a high speed, and was killed instantly. He actually had become the first fatality on the brand new Turner Turnpike that had just opened between Tulsa and Oklahoma City.

In 1953, there were no seat belts in cars. Seat belts were not offered until Ford offered a lap belt as an option in 1955. Saab was the first to install them as standard equipment in 1958. You can imagine hitting a bridge support column head-on would have been very bad. To make matters worse, they later said that the smashed speedometer in the dash of the car was pinned at 80 mph.

I ran out the back door of the house and to the steps of the building in the back yard that housed my father's office at home. It was set up for him to do remote radio broadcasts in the event his schedule was too tight to get to the office at church. I sat alone on the steps and cried. I could not imagine how a loving God could let this happen to my dad. After all, he was a legend in terms of doing good works and helping people.

He placed over 500 children in good Christian homes by adoption through his Beams of Light Orphanage. He started numerous churches in several towns and other states outside Tulsa, Oklahoma. He was the modern version of the old circuit-riding preacher, except that when he went from church to church, instead of riding a horse, he flew his Cessna 172. He was asked to run for Governor of Oklahoma with offered financial support and campaign help, but he refused. He said he was called to the ministry. Because he was a notable radio broadcaster, he was invited to attend the initial formation meeting for establishing the National Religious Broadcasters (NRB). He was even a first Board Member of the NRB, an organization that survives today. Why didn't he survive? He was only 45. I know God is in control, but this was hard for me to handle.

Some say my dad lived an extraordinary life, because he accomplished more in 45 years than most men accomplish in a lifetime. While that is probably true, that argument does nothing to put salve in the wounds of losing my father in a premature death. I could only be angry at God for "taking him home," as the funeral service speakers said. I felt I needed a dad more in our home than God needed him at His "home." It took me years to get over my dad's death when I was only age 12. I looked up to him … I respected him … I admired him … I missed him. As a son, I believe my dad was the greatest example of a Godly man … the best … and I was fortunate to have him.

My dad was 100% sold out to serving God. In fact, if you visit his grave in Tulsa, you will see the verse he asked to be placed on his tombstone to summarize his life; Philippians 1:21, *"For to me to live is Christ, and to die is gain."*

# ORIGIN: THE GENE POOL

*"Children's children are the crown of old men;*
*and the glory of children are their fathers."* Proverbs 17:6

Because my dad died in an auto accident when I was age 12, I never spoke to him about his history and interests. I would have been interested in knowing those things, as it related to my own interests.

Where did my interest in politics come from? Not everyone has that interest; yet, I did. I attended monthly meetings of my political party, and I was elected as District Officer in Georgia. I was elected as one of Georgia's 40 delegates to the National Convention of the Republican Party in 1988 in New Orleans. I was elected as one of the 48 State delegates for Georgia to the 1996 National Convention in San Diego. I have often wondered where that interest in politics came from. I even had men in my county come to me pledging their support if I would run for office in the Georgia State House of Representatives. I declined because I was afraid I would win and then be stuck in the "box" of the State Capital Building listening to dull speeches, arguments and filibusters. I knew of no elected family members to public office in my history.

I got my answer to my interest in politics when my mother passed away, and we were going through hundreds of records in her file cabinets. My mother never threw anything out. In one cabinet was a file of letters to my dad that pledged support and asked him to run for Governor of Oklahoma. Also in that file were copies of his reasons against running. Even though he thought he would win, it was not what he was *called* to do. He said he was "called by God" to preach, as this was his purpose in life on earth.

49

Where did my interest in renovating rental properties come from? I left my stockholder position with Merrill Lynch to raise money by syndication to buy apartments, fix them up, manage them, and sell them for a profit for the investors. For years, the investors had each received over 100% return *per year* on their investments in my real estate syndications. However, I had no other family member in history doing real estate investments. Where did my drive to do that come from?

Again, I got my answer from the files of my mother. There were records of run-down homes in Bristow, Oklahoma, that my father had purchased, fixed up, and sold for a profit. This was how he supported the family while he was starting his first church ministry in Bristow, until the church became large enough to support a full time pastor and before he moved his ministry, church and orphanage to Tulsa.

From where did I get my interest and inclinations toward law? When I had lawsuits from the real estate debacle arising from the Tax Reform Act of 1986, I successfully acted as my own legal defense. I had never had any legal training. I never lost a case either. Now, where did that interest and ability come from?

Again, I got my answers from the files my mother had kept. In one file, I found a case where my father was driving over a hill when a school bus stopped just over the hill with disembarking children. My father hit a child getting off the bus that had run out in front of his car. The records showed my father handled his own defense in court. He was exonerated as "Not Guilty." The legal mind must be in the genes.

I can now see why, in early history, many children became apprentices under their fathers, uncles, or other family members as they learned their trade. A tour through Williamsburg, Virginia, will tell you that in early times of our country, apprenticeships are how leather craft, brick making, barrel staves, brewing, or farming was passed down to the next generation. Nowadays, it shows up often in politician sons of politicians, or athletic sons of great athletes. I know that many of my natural inclinations came to me naturally from my father, without him working with me, or even talking to me about them.

Proverbs 17:6 says, *"Children's children are the crown of old men; and the glory of children are their fathers."* I suppose that if we studied what our fathers liked to do, we would have a better understanding of our own inclinations and ourselves. It is probably not the exact job, but those skills and desires of our fathers should be considered when choosing a desired occupation today.

As I write this, I am the Executive Director of Faith Farm Ministries, a drug and alcohol addiction recovery ministry. Faith Farm provides a free, residential recovery program for 445 men and women. I always wondered why I consider this the best job I have ever had, since I have never done this type of work in several past CEO positions. I just love to see lives helped and changed. This part of the "gene pool" is easy to see. My father loved taking care of the children in his orphanage. He loved to see their lives remade through a loving environment, and subsequently placed in a home via adoption, where they would be loved, nurtured and wanted. Now, my work is helping men and women break drug and alcohol addictions. They spiritually renew their lives, and receive job training and help with their education. Our motto, "A ministry with a Heart for the Hurting" and our tag line, "Restoring Hope, one life at a time" sure fits in with that "gene pool" heart of giving a helping hand.

I have had the extraordinary discovery of my father's "DNA" as I lived my life, without being aware of my father's life, until my mother passed away and we read the files in her home office. My life is evident in Proverbs 17:6, *"... and the glory of children are their fathers."*

# NO STUDENT LOANS

*"Go therefore now, and work."* Exodus 5:18
*"If any would not work, neither should he eat."* II Thessalonians 3:10

It had been a dream of mine to be one of the first members of my family to graduate from college and to get a college degree. I had neither the athletic ability nor specialty intellect to earn a scholarship. Another handicap was that my father died in an automobile accident on Thanksgiving Day when I had just turned age 12. We had no savings or college funds of any kind. In addition, pastors were not part of the Social Security system until 1951, leading up to the time of my father's death in 1953, and my father had not yet signed up to be admitted into the system. Therefore, there was no safety net for my mom and our family. If I were to do it, I would have to work my way through college entirely on my own.

I looked at all the schools in Tulsa where I lived and all over Oklahoma. Oklahoma State University in Stillwater, Oklahoma, seemed the best fit. I headed 80 miles West of Tulsa to Stillwater, in my 10-year old used car. I had purchased it with money I saved while bagging groceries at the local grocery stores after high school classes. I looked for every job I could find to earn money.

To get a room in the men's dormitory, West Bennett Hall, I exchanged the total room and board allowance for my services. I became a counselor who walked the halls in the evenings to keep it quiet for the students to study, in exchange for my room costs. I kept a portion of the food allowance to use in the dorm cafeteria for breakfast and exchanged the lunch and dinner allowance for cash to buy my books. I also waited tables in a family-style boarding house that was one block from campus in exchange for my lunch, and then waited tables and washed dishes at the Delta Delta Delta (Tri-Delta) Sorority in exchange for my evening meal. In between lunch and dinner, I was a disc jockey and news announcer on KOSU-FM, the University's campus radio station. After I washed the Tri-Delta dishes, I raced back to my dorm for my hall monitor (Counselor) job. On weekends, I drove 80 miles back to Tulsa and worked Saturdays and Sundays as a sales clerk at Sears, and then drove the 80 miles back to Stillwater on Sunday evening to start the week all over again.

I do not have any fond memories of college days. I felt like I was in a mode of slave labor. I worked every hour that I was not in class, leaving little time to study. There certainly was no time for any social life whatsoever. I was always exhausted. I remember going into one essay-type, final exam. When the professor said "Start," I began writing. An hour later the professor woke me up shaking my shoulder. When I lifted my face up off the desk, exposing my blue essay book, I had only started and written one line, not even finishing the first sentence. That is how exhausted I was. Fortunately, I had done well on my other exams throughout the semester. Therefore, even with that zero on the final, I still got a "C" in the course.

That event pretty much describes my college days. I was always envious of my classmates who had time to socialize, date, and engage in deep conversations. I only had time to work, go to class, study and sleep 3-4 hours per night. I lived on "No-Doze," a caffeine-charged tablet to keep me awake.

However, I MADE IT! I graduated in four years from a State University with no benefit of student loans, grants, or scholarships. I never worked so hard in all my life on so many jobs at once. I majored in Marketing with a minor in Speech. Without my degree, I would never have been able to do so many meaningful things in my life. For example, I was a stockbroker with Merrill Lynch in New York. I attended the U.S. Naval War College in Newport, Rhode Island. I was commissioned in the Navy, which allowed me the opportunity to reach the rank of Commander. Finally, the CEO jobs I have had that have required a college degree have meant so much to me.

I proved to myself that I could do anything I wanted to do if I would work hard enough at it and apply myself. Having no savings, student loans, grants or scholarships made my accomplishments much harder, but also more rewarding. Looking back, my hard work through college is one of the things that I am most proud of, and it gives me the greatest sense of accomplishment. Now that I hear about staggering college loan debt, even above scholarships obtained, I feel an even greater sense of accomplishing something extraordinary. At least I certainly lived out Exodus 5:18, which says, *"Go therefore now, and work ..."*

# KOSU-FM

I was a student disc jockey at KOSU-FM, the on-campus radio station of Oklahoma State University (OSU), during my sophomore year. During my afternoon D.J. time, I was usually alone and responsible for operating the entire studio, including doing the hourly news broadcast.

One day during the show, I needed to use the restroom. I took a call-in request for a song, selected the requested 45, slapped it on the turntable, and dropped the arm and needle at the edge to begin the song play. I then raced for the studio door, propped it open so I could get back in (the door was self-locking) and raced down the hall to the bathroom. The goal, of course, was to finish going to the restroom and return before the requested song finished playing.

As I was standing at the urinal, the horror of realizing that I had put the wrong side of the requested 45-RPM record on the turntable overwhelmed me as the program broadcast through speakers in all the common areas, including the bathrooms. It was instantly painful as I heard a robust, German beer-garden group, complete with accordions, bellowing out:

> "Just give me beer, beer, and more beer,
> I just love that foamy stuff.
> Just give me beer, beer, and more beer,
> I just cannot seem to get enough.
> So if you want to make me happy,
> Then brother lend an ear.
> I will tell you what to do,
> Just go and get some brew,
> And give me beer, beer, and more beer."

I had waited way too long to use the restroom, there was nothing I could do to shut it down. I had to listen to the whole song and all its verses sung twice through, before I could race back down the hall to the studio. It was too late to stop it, and it had just about played to the end. I noticed the phone lines were blinking, especially the station manager's "hot line," which always had to be answered immediately by simply muting my mic and taking his call. This time, I queued up the correct side of the requested record on the turntable to begin immediately upon the completion of the beer-garden song. Then, I took the call.

Sure enough, the manager was mad, as he should have been. I was tasked with playing "easy listening" music during the afternoons, when students were (supposed to be) studying. I was allowed to take phone-in requests, but only honoring the "easy listening" genre suitable for quiet study time. I explained the honest mistake, and that it would not happen again. The most amazing thing to me is I was so traumatized and pumped up by a flood of adrenaline; I instantly memorized all the words above in just one hearing of it.

Luckily, the manager was not listening during the prank my fellow students pulled on me a different day. As part of my duties as the D.J., I also did the 5-minutes of news each hour. A single mic hung from the ceiling in the middle of the round newsroom, which I accessed through a thick, soundproof door from my D.J. studio. There was a constant feed of news over the teletype machine. As it got closer to news time, while the records played, I would read all the typed news, and with a black magic marker, simply strike out stories of little local interest. I would estimate what news I could get through in five minutes of scheduled news time. I would tear the 10-15 foot long paper away from the teletype; turn on the mic in the adjoining "news studio," and stand in the middle of the room under the mic in the center. I would read the news, skipping those items I had placed an "X" through, and ending as close to 5 minutes of news as I could.

I never shut the huge, soundproof door between my D.J. studio with the music consol and the newsroom, allowing me to run into the adjoining studio to read the news, and get back to my D.J. consol quickly.

One afternoon while I was steadily reading the news on the 10-foot length of teletype paper, I smelled smoke. It seems my "friends" had slipped into the D.J. studio, and then into the adjoining news studio. They had taken a cigarette lighter, lit the bottom edge of the long teletype paper, and it was burning. As the flame began to catch and rise, I began to read the news faster and faster. The flames began to creep up my pages, burning more and more of the news stories I was yet to read. I could not stop reading because the broadcast was live. I was very fortunate to get through almost 5 minutes of scheduled news time before I ran out to the music studio, switched on the mics, and began to play the next record I had queued up. I then raced back into the news studio and began stomping out the paper fire. I was so glad the building did not have a sprinkler system in it, because of the damage the water would have done. I would have been fired! Somehow, I managed to get through that prank without any call from the manager or feedback from any listeners.

Although these were extraordinary experiences for this naïve, Oklahoma boy, I suppose it was a milder prank than most college pranks I have heard about. However, it sure was stressful to me.

# LORD, YOU WANT ME TO GO WHERE?

*"Trust in the Lord with all thine heart: and lean not
unto thine own understanding. In all thy ways acknowledge Him,
and He shall direct thy paths."* Proverbs 3: 5 & 6

I was praying about a wife. I was between my sophomore year and my junior year in college. I had committed that summer to praying for a wife. I was very discouraged because of the "double standard" I was experiencing. However, it is not what you think. In the 1960's, the expected "double standard" was that boys would be the wild ones, and the girls were expected to stop any errant activity and set the moral standard for any relationship. I had committed to being a moral man until marriage, but I was having trouble with the girls I was dating in college. *They* seemed to be the wild ones! I was looking for, but not finding, a girl with the same moral values that I was committed to live by.

That summer, every time I got on my knees to pray, I kept feeling an urging to go to a particular school that I did not want to attend.  My older sister had gone to that school in Greenville, South Carolina, so I had seen the school when we visited her. I had finished two years as a sophomore at Oklahoma State University. I sure did not want to move from a school of over 25,000 students and go to a small school of under 3,000. The main reason was that I did not like the school. It had many rules. I did not want to be restricted to living by strict rules and confining regulations.

When I told my mother what was happening day after day when I prayed, she simply asked, "What are you praying about when you get the feelings that you should go to that school?" I told her I was "praying about a wife." She wisely said that maybe I was

61

getting my answer to prayer, and that I should consider going there. "Maybe that was where I would meet my wife," she said.

It was already late summer. Acting on my mother's comment, I applied and that school accepted me. My younger sister, Ruth, said that since she was looking for a college to enter and since I was changing to that school, then maybe she would go with me. She applied, and off we drove to Greenville, South Carolina, together.

At that school, they have a large "dining common" where the entire student body sits at tables, at one time, to be served their meals. Each table has a host or hostess. The table I happened to pick had a hostess, who was a senior about to graduate at mid-term in the next four months. I really did not think much about her since she was graduating. Other than that, she had a wonderful personality, and she was very clever and funny. I even thought her name was funny: "Bertie."

I told the table about my experience that first afternoon. Earlier that day, I was driving off campus to go to a movie before dinner. The guard stopped me at the campus exit gate, and he asked where I was going. When I said, "To the movies," he dropped the gate, blocked my exit, and asked me to get out of the car. He immediately gave me a Pink Slip for leaving campus without written permission. (I never had to get "permission" to leave campus at Oklahoma State.) Then, he wrote another Pink Slip for attempting to go to a movie. I was surprised to find out going to a movie was also forbidden. Then, he noticed that I was wearing shorts. He wrote another Pink Slip for not being "properly dressed." I had no idea how critical it was to make reading the Rule Book a top priority. I had been on campus less than three hours and already had three Pink Slips for rule violations to report to the

Dean of Men's office the next morning. Wow! I was going to start my very first class late. The group seated at my first dining table experience had a great laugh at the story of the "new guy" and his utter naïveté.

Later that night at the evening meal, Bertie, the table hostess, found out that this was my first night on campus and invited me down to her dorm for "watermelon." She gave me the name of her dormitory. I thought this was pretty cool. I left the dining hall and began to walk across campus to the women's dorm name she gave me. The campus cops soon stopped me and gave me a "Pink Slip." I was to report to the Dean of Men the next morning before classes. It seems that the men's dorms are on one side of the campus, and the women's dorms are on the opposite side of campus. It is a "felony" to ever venture over to the female side of campus. While Bertie may have thought it was cute (she admitted so later), I now had FOUR Pink Slips and had to report to the Dean of Men before my first morning's first class. My first 12 hours on campus, I got so many "demerits" that I was restricted from leaving campus for over a month. I was beginning to feel like one of those missionaries who went into a horrible mission field environment. They did not want to go, but went anyway out of an "urging" in prayer in obedience to God. At least I was in South Carolina and not some place in Africa.

On Sunday morning, church was mandatory, but Sunday school was "optional". Being new and not knowing the ropes, I stayed in my room during Sunday school hours, straightened up, and shined my shoes. A hall monitor came by and asked why I was not in Sunday school. I said I was shining my shoes and was going to Sunday morning service when I finished. To my surprise, the monitor returned with a Pink Slip for missing Sunday school. I said,

"I thought Sunday school was optional." He said, "It is, but the mere fact I chose not to go showed that I had a "spiritual problem," and I needed to report to the Dean of Men before class in the morning." I was late to yet another Monday morning class and was grounded for yet another month and unable to leave campus.

Meanwhile, my sister, Ruth, kept calling the dorm to speak to me. Family members were the only females allowed to call. She kept telling me about this great girl in her dorm that I should ask for a date. She said her name was "Bertie." I said "On no! I've been done in by that girl already, and I will never be around her again." I would not listen to her pleas. I dated 17 different girls there before I asked Bertie out. A "date" meant that you could go to a church service, "Vespers", a Sunday afternoon musical or other special entertainment, and the snack shop. At monitored times; you could walk the "snail trail," which was the chaperoned dating line down the sidewalk to their dorm's front door, as long as you kept a 12-inch space between shoulders. The first time I walked the dating line, I got a Pink Slip for wedging a 12-inch ruler between our shoulders and leaning in to hold it there. They did not appreciate my attempt at humor. I just did not seem to be able to fit into the very controlled, restrictive culture.

I finally asked Bertie out to an event on campus, and she was fun. In fact, since she was a senior, she was always in a "supervisory" position. For example, they had a "Dating Parlor" above the snack shop where you could go after church or other events. It was a huge room full of sofas, like a massive furniture store containing only sofas. Couples would sit at opposite ends of the sofas and talk to their dates. One evening, Bertie was walking down the steps with me, and she told me to count the steps, because between the floors, there were three steps, blocked from line of sight because of a support beam, and you could not see someone's head from the bottom of the stairs. Nor could the Dating Monitor see someone's head from the top of the stairs from way back where he sat. I needed no more ideas... I counted steps and grabbed my first kiss with Bertie. She was cool.

As you can imagine, I was kicked out of that school. They called it being "shipped." I was shipped five days before the end of my first semester. Someone accused me of gathering up a group to stand up to the administration in a revolt about the rules (not true). Since I spent more time in the Dean's office than in class or on campus, I am not exactly sure how I could do that. In fact, I lived in such fear, I barely spoke to anyone for fear I would say something wrong. I went to a hotel for five days to wait for my sister, Ruth, to finish the semester. She was leaving, too, and she wanted to ride back to Oklahoma with me. Since Bertie was graduating and was free now, she took a cab to see me, and we really connected. It was so much fun to be around her.

After I left and returned to Tulsa, I kept in touch with Bertie. We wrote and called almost every day. I returned to Oklahoma State University. They said they had a policy about not readmitting anyone who was kicked out of another university. They asked me which one, and I told them. They said, "Oh, that's different. You can come back." (I never figured out how they knew enough about that culture to let me back in because I never said anything to OSU

Admissions about that school and its restrictive policies.) They said they thought that Billy Graham was kicked out of there, too, so I was in "good company."

After I graduated, I was drafted in the Army, so I pre-empted that by enlisting in Officer Candidate Flight School for the Navy. Bertie and I decided it was cheaper to get married than to keep trying to pay the airline bills and phone bills we were paying to try to be together. Bertie and I became "ONE" and inseparable until she died 32 years later of breast cancer.

I was so glad I listened to the "still small voice" of God to go to a school I did not want to go to, in order to meet my wife, as my mom so wisely predicted. Through this extraordinary experience, I was learning to trust God when I prayed without knowing all the details. As Proverbs 3:5-6 says, "*Trust in the Lord with all thine heart, and lean not on thine own understanding. In all thy ways acknowledge Him, and He shall direct thy paths.*" That is very true!

# ASKING FOR HER HAND

*"Ask, and it shall be given you."* Matthew 7:7

Sitting on the couch was R.C. Rigdon, with his 6 foot 4 inch frame leaning over with his hands clasped in front of him, while staring at me with those piercing eyes. I was sitting on the couch against the opposite wall, facing him. I could not have been any more intimidated. He was a powerful executive, Vice President of the Winn Dixie grocery store chain, and I was there to ask for his daughter's hand in marriage. I had never been so nervous. We just did not have to do this sort of thing in Tulsa, but Bertie said it was required in a good southern family in Raleigh, North Carolina. I had driven 27 hours over a 3-day weekend to ask for his daughter's hand in marriage. It did not help that I was recalling a time when I had called Bertie on the phone. Her Dad answered, and I overheard him announce to her that the call was for her from "that thing in Oklahoma."

Now, that "thing" was sitting on the couch across from him. My heart was in my throat, and I feared for my life because my heart was pounding so hard. Although I had rehearsed in my mind a hundred times what I was going to say, when I reached this point, my mind was blank.

As he continued to stare at me, beads of sweat began to build on my forehead. Finally, I blurted out some staccato string of words that included something about how I loved his daughter and was asking for his permission for me to ask her to marry me.

To make matters worse, there was no change in his stoic expressionless face when I finished my outburst. Finally, when he spoke, he said, "The only problem with that is you're not good enough for my daughter." He then just continued to stare at me. The silence was deafening.

*OK ... so what do I do now? Do I start arguing that even though I am from Oklahoma, I am good enough; that I did have my life planned out and the reasons why; that I was planning on going into the Naval Officer Candidate School to be a Naval Officer; that I was then planning on going to New York to become a stockbroker? What could I say to be "good enough?"*

The long lapse of silence seemed like an eternity, while the various thoughts were racing through my mind that I was going to use to defend myself, he broke the ice with a smile. He leaned forward, extending his hand for a handshake, and said, *"But then, nobody would be."*

A ton of weight lifted off my shoulders as I extended my hand to shake his. "Welcome to the family," he said.

Now, why would anyone have to go through this for an engagement? I grew up in Oklahoma, in the land of Will Rogers, Garth Brooks, and T. Boone Pickens, where we kept life plain and simple. I am glad I got through this, and I never want to do it again. However, it was worth it for the 32 years of incredible bliss I had with Bertie before she passed away. She was worth it all. As Matthew 7:7 says, *"Ask, and it shall be given you."*

# WEDDING NIGHT SCARE

*"She will do him good and not evil all the days of her life."* Proverbs 31:12

Finally, the wedding festivities were over. The cake cutting, reception line, photos, tossing the bouquet, and all the other formalities and festivities concluded. Now, we are getting to the "main course," at least what I have been waiting for all my life … the wedding night. To those who have not "saved themselves" for their eventual first marriage partner, this was more than likely not monumental to them. However, to those of us raised and taught to exercise the self-discipline to be virgins on our wedding night, this was a big deal. To those of us who had exercised sexual restraint our whole lives against desires and urges … this was a huge deal. The thought of finally making love to the love of your life made each extra minute of the expected "necessary" wedding festivities seem like ten.

We finally reached the bridal suite bungalow at the Plantation Inn and opened the door. To our shock, there was my brother-in-law, Ken, sitting in the middle of the white canopied bed with the silver tray of sweets I had ordered … and he was eating them. I do not know how he found out where we were going to stay, or even how he gained access to our bridal suite, but this was not funny. I was not at all amused. It took a lot of passion with raised voice and pleading, to persuade him to leave. We were not receptive to his "joke" at all.

Finally, we were alone and turned around, each opening our luggage to get the appropriate clothing to don after showers. We were about to begin the part of the day I had been looking forward to for 23 years. Bertie said, "Dean, I want to say something to you."

I turned around and she dug down into her suitcase below her clothing and negligees' and pulled out a huge pair of hedge clippers. She began snapping the blades together as if she was trimming a hedge in front of her. I was shocked and not at all sure about what was going on, but the staccato sound of the sharp metal-on-metal blades scraping each other as she repeatedly snapped them open and shut sent a chill up my spine. She let the shock on my face remain only so long before she stopped snapping the shears together and spoke. "Honey," she said, "I'll be there for you anytime you want it, as often as you want it, wherever you want it. It will be willingly and with passion. I am at your beck and call … anytime … anywhere. But, if I ever find out that you've cheated on me, sooner or later you'll have to fall asleep, and I'll make sure you'll wish you never cheated on me." She said, "My mother told me to always keep my man happy at home, and he'd never want to sample the goods elsewhere." Then she stopped snapping the blades closed, and put them away. Suddenly it was quiet again. Wow … It was a very sobering, unforgettable, heart-pounding moment.

She kept her bargain, and I kept mine. I never, ever, in over 32 years of marriage, even thought about anyone else. I could not … she kept me exhausted. In retrospect, I can only suppose that if I ever had other thoughts of straying, I probably would have had those thoughts killed by the image and sound of those snapping hedge clipper blades. It made an indelible impression on me. It was a wonderful mutual agreement, and a partnership that continued to flourish for over 32 years until she died of cancer. She was an unusual gem …. She was one of a kind. As Proverbs 31:12 says, *"She did me good and not evil all the days of her life."*

Our Wedding Day

# NAVY JOB SELECTION MIRACLE

*"A good man obtaineth favor of the Lord."* Proverbs 12:2

My hands were sweating as I stood in line. My class of 82 men were about to get our commissions in the U.S. Navy. We stood in line in the order of our academic finish in our class to select our choice of aircraft to fly. Unfortunately, I was not a wiz in math, electronics, or systems, so I finished 79th out of 82. Only three people were behind me, and 78 classmates were ahead of me. We were in line to go into the operations building to select where we were going to be stationed based upon what type of plane we selected to fly. They had only so many planned openings in each type of aircraft all written on a large chalkboard, so you selected from what was available. If the opening you desired was gone, you had to select your choice out of what was remaining. Only 82 choices were available, and 78 of them would be gone by the time I got my chance at selection.

The reason I was sweating it so much was our class was divided between "fighters" and "lovers." Some were just itching to get into action on the aircraft carriers and go into combat in jet fighters and attack aircraft. On the other hand, some of us were lovers, and wanted to go on transports, which carry troops and supplies … you know … room in the plane to walk around, bathrooms, cook your dinner, land-based aircraft … no cramped quarters for us on a ship, but land-based officer quarters were what we wanted. Everyone seemed to know what the best choices were for them before lining up. The only problem was that there were many times more open slots on fighters than on transports. After all, we were at war in Vietnam.

Because I wore eyeglasses, I could not be a pilot. However, with corrected vision to 20/20, I could fly as a Navigator. We had choices such as F-8's, F4B Phantoms, and the safe, stodgy transports. That is what I wanted. I did not desire to straddle a jet engine behind a pilot, wear a G-suit, and have to speak against unbelievable air pressure shoved down my throat through a mask strapped over my face while I tried to talk clearly. In a fighter aircraft, as you spoke your words, you had to do so while you were forcing air out of your lungs with enough pressure to overcome the incoming air pressure... and be able to speak clearly enough to be understood by the tower or another aircraft. Well, I wanted to leave that for the fighters; the "jet jocks." Me ... I was a lover, not a fighter. I was here only because I was drafted. I had gone to Dallas from Tulsa to sign up in Officer Candidate School just as soon as I was drafted to avoid being a "ground pounder" in a foxhole in the Army. In fact, I jumped off the draftee induction bus heading to Oklahoma City to be given our physicals, and flew to Dallas to sign up for the Naval Officer Candidate and Flight school.

As the first guys came out passed the waiting line, of course everyone was asking what was available. We "lovers" were asking about transport slots. They said that only six slots were initially available, and two were taken within the first ten guys in line. The odds of me getting what I wanted were beyond setting odds. They were ridiculous odds.

I will never forget when one of my classmates came out saying "I got the last transport." My heart sank, and my mind was going crazy. I could not see myself being strapped into a pressure "G-suit" in the rear seat of an attack aircraft, hooked up to a catapult on the Aircraft Carrier, and being shot off the end of the ship like a cannon, while pulling 26 G's on the shot. Then, flying over enemy territory and navigating to a target, to drop our ordinance, working a relative motion problem back to find our launching Carrier in the ocean, and landing on a postage stamp size target in the ocean. We would have our rear hook hanging down to catch the cable so we would not go off the bow of the ship and splash down in the ocean. I had seen enough of those movies of carrier launches and recovery to know I just did not see any advantage to having my runway to be only a block long, and rising and falling on the waves in the ocean. If I was going to be flying, I wanted to be landing on one of those stationary, 10,000 foot, non-moving landing strips on fixed land like the Air Force used. I did not choose one that is pitching up and down in the rough seas, rising and falling while you tried to hook a cable with your tail hook hanging while gliding or you would go over the edge. The Navy had taken this Orville and Wilbur Wright aviation thing to a ridiculous level.

My wife and I had prayed for weeks that I would get transports. If I was going to war in Vietnam anyway, we wanted the best chance for me to return alive. That chance, we believed, was me getting into transports. However, here I was, faced with the fact that transport selection opportunities were gone. Classmate after classmate came out of the building and down the line shaking their heads when we asked about transport slots. We knew they had been gone dozens of men earlier, but we still asked, hopefully. One by one, they told us the type of jet fighter they were forced to select from the options left.

I was sweating and my ears were ringing ... I was the next one in to select. I was praying under my breath. If I did not get transports, I did not care what type of jet attack or fighter plane I was assigned to. When I entered the office for my choice, several officers were on the phone, and the one up front asked me to choose. I looked at the giant board, and had two choices. Both were bad. I stalled, because I could not choose. I prayed under my breath, "Lord, what am I going to do?"

I cannot believe it all came down to this. Suddenly, one of the officers on the phone said, "We've got a new opening for a transport slot, so put it on the board." I shouted, "I'll take it!"

They wrote down the selection on my card, and I walked out to the last three guys and said, "I got transports." They could not believe it. Nor could I. God came through for me at just the last minute, just the exact right timing. Just a moment earlier or later and the cadet in front of me or behind me would have been able to make the selection. God really answered my prayers that day.

Over the next few years, over half of my classmates in that line were killed in Vietnam. I survived and traveled in transports to over 50 countries, and retired a Commander in the Naval Reserves. God was so good to me and had miraculously answered the prayers of my wife and me. As Proverbs 12:2 says, "... *obtained favor of the Lord.*" It was an extraordinary experience that made me feel I had *obtained favor,* and His timing was perfect. It was an obvious miraculous answer to our many prayers.

# AM I GOING TO DIE THIS WAY?

*"Because thou hast made the Lord, which is my refuge, even the most High, thy habitation; there shall no evil befall thee..."* Psalms 91: 9-10

My heart was in my throat. Our C-130 Transport was at 32,000 feet, and was being warned by Saigon Air Control. Looking out the cockpit window, we saw two Communist Chinese jets approaching head-on at us. At the last minute, they pulled up and climbed over us. Yes, chills went up my spine when I saw those heat-seeking SAM missiles hanging from wing tip to wing tip under both of those Chi-Com fighter jets. As the Navigator, I jumped up to raise the periscopic sextant through the upper skin of our aircraft that I used to obtain celestial fixes for navigational positioning. I swung it around to face the rear of the plane, and my blood turned to ice. The enemy jets were now turning and swinging in position behind us to be able to use their heat-seeking missiles on the jet exhaust of our Turboprop engines. We were dead ducks. We were an unarmed transport cargo plane powered by Turbo-prop engines ... jet engines to power our props ... just the kind of engine those heat-seekers were designed for ... to hone in and fix on our heat exhaust. I thought *"Oh my God. I'm going to die on my very first flight to Vietnam."*

I had completed navigation training, received my Navy Navigator flight wings, and this was my first navigation in real life, wartime conditions ... a cargo mission to Vietnam. Of course, we have live navigation training flights over the Gulf of Mexico before we get our wings, but this was my first time to navigate in a real, wartime scenario. As was customary, the first time a new navigator is in a real situation, that new navigator is accompanied by a navigation instructor. I will call mine, "Louie." Louie had been asleep on the bunk on the flight deck, next to my navigation table. Evidently, he really trusted me, because he was sleeping and believed there was no need to be alarmed or concerned. Because it was a day flight, I only had the sun to get a clean "line of position" with my sextant, unlike the night, when you can get a "fix" by shooting three stars 120-degrees apart. These three lines of position form a triangle when you plot it on the charts, and your assumed "fixed" position is in the middle of the triangle. Since I only had a single line of position from the sun that we could place on the navigation chart, and not a fixed position, the pilot broke radio silence and asked Saigon Air for our position coordinates for me to plot. When I plotted it, it fell right on my last single line of position. The only trouble was that although it *was* on the line, it was 200 miles north of where we were supposed to be. Being there meant we had violated Communist Chinese airspace by getting too close to their most southerly island, Hainan. Therefore, they scrambled the two fighter jets with missiles. As the navigator giving headings to the pilot, I had unknowingly caused us to violate their sovereign air space.

Because Saigon Air knew we were in deep trouble due to our position, and the fact that two missile-armed fighter jets were behind us, Saigon advised us to begin making a slow descent, while turning South away from the Hainan Island and lowering our speed as we lowered our altitude. This maneuver dispelled the perception of us being a threat to the Chinese. I quickly got a radar fix and saw on the navigation charts that the curved outline shape of the shoreline of where we were intending to cross over land looked exactly like the curvature of the Chinese Hainan Island on my global navigation chart. Therefore, I did not notice anything that looked unusual to me on my radarscope. In addition, I am sure they did not feel comfortable with an unidentified aircraft at our altitude and speed, "painting" their coastline with our radar.

As a new navigator, I had made an egregious error that could have gotten us all killed … needlessly. After we slowed, turned away from the Island and descended, the Chinese jets peeled off and headed back to their island base. They knew that at our ever-decreasingly lower altitude, our jet-turboprops would be burning so much fuel, that we would not be a threat to turn around toward their island or mainland again, and still be able to return to whatever base we were going to … safely. The lower altitude caused them to also burn more fuel, so they had to return to their base. Saigon Air knew exactly what to do to diffuse the situation and save us. I have never been so scared in my life. And, poor Louie got a reprimand for sleeping through this and not checking up on the new navigator's work on my first real-life, real-time flight around enemy territory.

I do not know if you have ever been in a position that you really thought you were going to die. I can tell you that what they say is true … Your whole life really does flash before you. With the adrenalin shooting through my body, the tape of my life sped through my mind in split seconds. I thought of all the things I could not do if I were shot out of the sky. I thought of my wife and daughter left behind, and how they would take the news of my death. I thought of all the things I could not undo: words of kindness that could have and should have been said; hurtful words I would like to take back; decisions that might have been made differently. All I can do is advise you (and me, too) to live your life every day so you have no regrets. We were never promised tomorrow.

Although I lived through this extraordinary experience, I would not want to repeat it. Psalms 91:9-10 does say, *"Because thou hast made the Lord, which is my refuge, even the most High, thy habitation; There shall no evil befall thee..."*

# OLONGAPO CITY

*"Surely He will deliver thee... from the noisome pestilence."*   Psalms 91:3

In the blackest night, I lay in the hotel bed and awakened, surrounded by hearing scratching sounds on the walls. Cold chills ran down my spine, wondering if it was what I thought it was. I was too afraid to turn on the lamp beside my bed to confront the sounds visually.

I was the navigator, a crewmember on a C-130 crew staging from the U.S. into Vietnam. Our last stopover before going into Vietnam was the Navy base in the Philippines near Olongapo City for refueling and sleep. Olongapo City was 79 miles north of Manila and bordered by mountains, Subic Bay Naval Base, and Subic Bay, in the Province of Zambales. There were so many Vietnam support cargo flights passing through the base that the enlisted and officer quarters were full. Therefore, they sent us on per diem allowances to find food and lodging in Olongapo City for the night. That was an interesting venture. We took a military bus from the base into Olongapo City. It was an old bus and not air-conditioned. All the windows were lowered to catch a breeze against the sweltering heat. As we wound through the curves of the old road into town, we passed dozens of Philipinos standing along the roadside over grills holding up skewers of meat yelling, "GI Joe, Monkey Meat. GI Joe, Monkey Meat." We did not stop to eat.

Olongapo catered to thousands of servicemen coming into town for a break from the warfare. Just picture a western town in a movie, with dirt streets, buildings on both sides, and no automobiles. Bars lined the streets, where loud bands played and imitated their favorite American idolized bands. Attractive Philipino girls belted out songs in English that they had memorized from recordings to sound exactly like the U.S. recording star, even though they could not speak a word of English themselves and did not even know what they were singing. They had just perfectly memorized and imitated the American songs and sounds. Servicemen were connecting with bar maids and prostitutes, staggering drunkenly through the streets, void of automobiles. We were concerned about finding good, clean, edible food to eat in that town. Our flight crew spotted a U.S. franchised pizza parlor, which we decided was the safest food and environment to try to eat. We went upstairs to the pizza parlor on the second floor over a bar and sat down to order our pizza. There were six of us sitting at a round table back in the corner of a dimly lighted room. Being an American pizza chain, at least the menus were in English. We hoped the food would be as Americanized as possible. We were beginning to feel a little bit relieved.

Less than two minutes after the waitress brought us menus, but before we even had time to read them, an attractive young woman in a silver, sequined dress slowly walked over to our table. She stood in front of the aircraft commander, asked him to turn his chair around, stood at his knees and unzipped the hidden, full-length dress zipper. The dress fell to the floor. Instantly standing buck naked, she stepped up, straddled the officer's legs, and sat down on his legs facing him. She asked in broken English, "Is there anything I can do for you?"

Are you kidding me ... In an American franchised pizza parlor? Was there no safe place in this town? It was worse than any bar-room saloon scene in the Wild West movies I had seen.

Welcome to Olongapo! It appeared that there were no restraints at all in that town. We immediately got rid of her so we could order our pizza. She was offended, but we did not care. The servicemen seated at the next table indicated to us that it was normal around there. They also indicated that they were going to search for a hotel immediately after they ate and advised us to do the same, before they all were gone, as there were limited rooms in the town. They reminded us that the Navy base should have told us that there was a 10:00 pm curfew, and anyone on the streets at that time would be arrested, even U.S. servicemen. As it got closer to 10:00, the servicemen pairing up with bar girls and prostitutes would be seeking beds for the night to get off the streets before curfew. The Philippine police had to institute early curfews because of the debauchery that progressed as the night went on. The drunken crime scene seemed to drop after they instituted the 10:00 pm curfews, so it became permanent.

Another thing the aircrew at the adjoining table cautioned us about when they found out this was our first time in Olongapo, was that we needed to stop and buy lighter fluid to carry to our hotel room. They recommended that we use that to protect us from roaches while we slept, and described how to use it. Therefore, we each bought some. We sought out rooms early, even though the "hotels" were all on the second floors above the bars and the loud music. You had to climb stairs between the bars to get to the "hotel" (and I use that term loosely). It was just a long hallway with rooms on each side.

Even though it was not yet dark or near the 10:00 pm police curfew, I knew I could not sleep because of the loud music below. I finally found a room to rent before they were all gone. The walls were paper thin, and I could hear activity sounds of servicemen with women in the adjacent rooms that I will not describe here.

The wallpaper in the room I rented had an old, red flocked velvet design, similar to what you would see in a Victorian mansion in days of old. As instructed by the Olongapo-experienced crewmembers at the adjacent table in the pizza parlor, I pulled the bed into the room, away from the walls. I placed each of the 4 iron post bed legs in the middle of a round disk of some sort (ashtray, jar lid, etc.) that would hold fluid. I then squirted lighter fluid in each container and positioned the bed leg to form a liquid moat of lighter fluid around each bed leg. They also instructed our table to be sure that no bed covers touched the floor. I climbed in. At 10:00 pm sharp, the loud music below stopped. Then, all I could hear were the sounds of couples in other rooms through the paper-thin hotel room walls, which was also disturbing. Eventually, all that stopped also, and I fell asleep.

After a few hours, I was awakened... not by any loud sound, but by very soft scratching sounds from all around me. Remembering the instructions and the very defensive preparations we were told to make, I still was afraid to turn on the light, but I did. What I saw made my heart jump.... Thousands, yes thousands, of giant 2 inch long roaches climbing all over the walls, making the red-flocked wall paper look like it had large black polka dots on it. In addition, the floor was covered with roaches. Lucky I did not have to use the bathroom. I could not have made it across the floor without stepping on many of them. I cannot even estimate how long it took me to finally fall back to sleep. I would not have if I had not been so exhausted. I had previously just completed a 10-hour navigation leg across the Pacific, so I was tired enough to fall back to sleep in this chaos.

I never wanted to visit Olongapo City again, and luckily, I never had to go back. One visit was extraordinary enough for me. Although I love to log a life full of unusual, extraordinary experiences, I can tell you I could have easily gone my whole life without that one.

NOTE:  If you go on the web to www.olongapocity.gov, the official website of Olongapo City, you will find that some 50 years later, Olongapo has paved roads and traffic circles with statuary and landscaping. Time changes things. In addition, on one road entering the city, there is a large, forest green archway over the road, which says, "Welcome, you are entering Olongapo City - Home of the most beautiful women in the world." (Then again, I guess some things never change.)

Retired U. S. Navy Commander, Dean O. Webb

# U.S. NAVAL WAR COLLEGE

*Whatsoever thy hand findeth to do,*
*do it with thy might.* Ecclesiastes 9:11

I saw an announcement for Naval Reserve Officers to apply for the 2-week Naval War College in Newport, Rhode Island. The course, "Defense Economics," was to be taught by Senior Naval Officers (Rear Admiral and above) and Senior Defense Civilians (Assistant Secretary of Defense and above). Out of thousands of officers, it was open to only 80 senior officers at the rank of Commander and above. I was only a Lt. Commander (equivalent to an Army or Air Force Major) at the time, but I was eligible for consideration for promotion to Commander just 2 weeks before the final War College roster selections. That was cutting it close, even if I DID make early promotion. I took a chance and applied. I had to argue for that consideration, reminding them that I was always promoted early and first. I hoped this next rank of Commander would be no exception. If so, I would make the War College deadline (barely), both time-wise and in minimum rank.

The applicants, many more than open spots available, all received a 10-inch high stack of recently declassified Department of Defense documents. From that, we were to write up a war contingency plan for various scenarios, using all air, ship, and missile assets, plus personnel inventory in all service branches. The plan had to be backed by a defense economic budget plan that encompassed all the scenarios of battle and budgets. Our dissertation plan, the equivalent of a Master's thesis, would be input into the naval war computer to see if it were feasible. If it worked, we would be in the pool and considered for selection to the War College, and then 80 officers would be selected to attend.

87

They gave a deadline of a certain final date at 5:00 pm to receive my thesis if it was to be considered.

The amazing thing is that I would work nights, parts of days, and all weekends for over 6 months on this project, knowing that to even be considered eligible, I was not high enough in rank as a senior officer. I would pour over all the various enemy attack points, set up defenses for all those attack scenarios utilizing all naval war assets and strengths, positioning submarine, carrier, warship and missile defenses to provide the ultimate defenses against all attack possibilities, and do it within my created defense budget. I would submit the thesis at the end of the 6 months work without knowing if I had even been promoted to Commander to be eligible to be considered, and then only if my war economic analysis thesis was acceptable. This was quite a gamble of invested time.

Meanwhile, I anxiously looked at the postings daily of the Pentagon Selection Board in Washington, D.C. to see if I had been selected for Commander. Finally, the promotion postings showed that I was selected for Commander. NOW, I was "officially" eligible for consideration and selection to the Naval War College in two weeks, IF my wartime footing budget passed the entire Admirals' scrutiny. I sent in my thesis to the War College and waited.

Two weeks later, I was accepted, based upon my work. I was the most junior officer ever attending the Naval War College, since I was promoted to the minimum rank of Commander barely in time to be eligible. I found out that I beat out a Rear Admiral for my slot because they did not receive his submission by the 5:00 pm deadline on the final date. I had sent mine via Federal Express to make sure they got mine on time. That small detail caused me to make it in time. Of course, we cannot forget the gutsy call to work for 6 months; nights, days, and weekends, not knowing if I were going to even be eligible based on my work; or, eligible contingent on making promotion just 2 weeks before the War College started; or, then to be selected from those eligible applicants. If you want something bad enough, go for it. You have to assume you are going to win. I have heard it said, "You have more good luck from hard work, than anything else I know." True.

Eccliastes 9:10 says, *"Whatsoever thy hand findeth to do, do it with thy might."*

After all the time, study and work on the economic thesis, it was worth it. Attending the U.S. Naval War College was one of the most incredible two weeks of my life. This life experience was extraordinary, as was the time gamble of 6 months hard work, not knowing if I was going to make rank early, or if my work would be acceptable to gain the acceptance invitation. Both had to occur for this to be experienced. It was an extraordinary gamble that worked!

Hanging over my desk, a shadowbox containing my Navy rank, Vietnam medals, dress sword and Navy Commander's Hat.

# CRAZY TED

I am sure we have all seen movies where military active duty servicemen are doing crazy antics. I suppose, at times, you have wondered if those types of actions can really be done without notice and some kind of consequence to the Navy sailor, Air Force or Army serviceman doing them. Regardless of how farfetched the actions seem, the stories have all been believable to me because of "*Crazy*" Ted.

Our Navy Air Transport Unit had a tall, broad shouldered, Greek, named Ted (I will not use his last name to protect him), who was a great pilot ... young, brash, and *crazy*. I say crazy because he did not particularly feel bound by rules. Nevertheless, he had proven himself enough an Aircraft Commander, even though young as lead pilots go. This meant he was the Lead Pilot and Captain over the whole Air Transport Crew, regardless of the rank of other Crew Member Officers (Co-pilots, Navigators, etc.)

Why did we call Ted, *Crazy*? U.S. Aircraft are supposed to remain at a minimum altitude of 500 feet above ground, unless in a takeoff or landing pattern. One day, we were out over the Atlantic Ocean at several thousand feet altitude, and Ted spotted a Russian Trawler all alone. He said, "Let's have some fun." Then, with no hesitation, he nosed over our huge, 4-engine, jet turbo prop, C-130 Transport into a dive, heading directly for the side of the Russian Trawler. As we got closer, we could see sailors on deck pointing up toward our aircraft. As we continued to get closer, we could see a couple of dozen sailors on deck running back and forth, waving their arms frantically. As we got even closer, they were all yelling and running back and forth in a panic. It reminded me of an old apartment I lived in once, when I pulled the refrigerator out of its spot, and the previously undisturbed roaches began running every which way ... in no particular direction. Sorry to say it, but this really was funny. Just prior to reaching the level of the top of the masts, Ted pulled the stick back so sharply that we could hear the engines stress as we pulled negative "G's" in our stomachs due to the abrupt change in altitude, as we pulled up our pitch from a dive to a level altitude. We safely cleared the ship masts at the bottom of our diving arch. We then skimmed the surface of the ocean to gain back airspeed until Ted began the climb back to altitude. We never told the Senior Officers about this episode, because we knew that blowing the whistle on Ted would get him reprimanded and maybe even court martialled. We kept quiet about the whole thing. As far as we knew, the incident was never reported.

Another time, Ted was the Aircraft Commander on one of our trips into Vietnam. During the Vietnam War, there were constant C-130 transport cargo trips into the war zone. Some carried cargo in and some carried caskets filled with casualties out. We would land in some place like Cam Ranh Bay, and while the loadmasters were discharging our cargo, reloading the C-130 cargo space, and refueling the plane, the pilots and navigator would be in flight ops getting weather briefings for the next route out to Japan and filing flight plans.

Ted told us to file the flight plan and he would get back to us in a couple of hours before scheduled takeoff time. Now, that was unusual, but we did not question it because *it was Ted.* After a couple of minutes, one of the crewmembers outside, who was attending to the refueling and reloading, came running into flight ops to tell us he had seen Ted dressing up in a "G-suit", the type that fighter pilots wear in fighter and attack aircraft. We went to where the crewmember said he saw Ted with the pilots, but they were not there.

We refueled and reloaded the C-130, filed the flight plan, checked the weather for the planned route, and got the latest small arms fire area. That was the area where Vietnamese soldiers were on the ground shooting at planes taking off or landing, hoping to hit a fuel tank, engine or somehow bring the aircraft down with small arms ground fire. Often, helicopter gunships would hover and strafe the woods to keep the enemy down, and keep them from being able to get a clear shot at the defenseless, fully loaded, huge 4-engine transports while taking off.

We paced for over an hour and it was time to go … and no Ted! Where was he? Suddenly someone yelled and pointed at an F-4 Phantom on a glide path to the runway, streaming smoke. The plane was riddled with bullets from the ground and was trailing smoke from several holes in the aircraft. They scrambled the ground rescue emergency crew, involving fire trucks and ambulances. We had never seen this type of emergency in the warzone, so we watched as the plane came to a stop. The fire engines sprayed down the aircraft with chemicals to put out whatever damage was causing the smoke, and to keep the fuel tanks from igniting. Finally, aircraft canopies opened, and the pilot and co-pilot began climbing down the ladders put up against the fuselage to the cockpit. As the two pilots reached the ground, they took off their helmets. We were shocked! The second pilot was Ted! Ted had gone on a short bombing run over enemy territory, while we were in filing our flight plans.

Again, we were mad at Ted. If he had not returned from the mission, he could have caused us to be stuck in the Vietnam warzone without a certified pilot to get us out of there. Our safety and ability to leave on the next leg of our mission would have been enough to have us stuck with no place to go, until the U.S. could get us another qualified transport pilot to continue. Once again, Ted had done something *crazy*, but because he returned from a successful mission in one piece, no one said anything. We were not even sure that the locals knew what happened. The pilot, using the unqualified Phantom "Pilot" Ted, would not have had a backup should he have been wounded on the mission. This was quite common. Often, the second pilot had to take control and land the fighter, if ground fire had wounded the lead pilot. This made us think that Ted's buddy letting him squeeze in this mission with him, while his crew was performing our required tasks, was probably *crazy*, too. In fact, servicemen in Vietnam felt that they were living just one day at a time, and could die at any time. They were often heavy drinkers and cavalier about relationships, because they always felt that they were such short-term encounters. They often felt like they were dead men walking. They were just waiting for their time to die.

Since we flew in transports and not in fighter or attack aircraft, we expected to return to our wives after each round robin cargo trip to Vietnam. Now, I *knew* that Ted was just *crazy* … He was in the "safest" way to fly in the warzone, yet he just took additional risks needlessly.

Another incident happened near our base in New Jersey. We were stationed at McGuire Air Force Base, an hour drive south of New York City. One of our training regimens was Combat Air Release Point (CARP) training. This was where we would load up the C-130 cargo area with military equipment, like tanks or jeeps. We would tie down the equipment on a wooded platform with a huge parachute attached. We would then practice air dropping them onto a target on the ground, simulating a wartime emergency airdrop behind enemy lines scenario. We would skim along at 500 feet altitude, simulating avoidance of enemy radar detection, and then pop up to 1,000 feet or more, open the rear bay door, and deploy the small chute at the navigator's signal. This would drag out the large parachute, and the wind would pull the platform containing the cargo out the back ramp to drop behind enemy lines for use by our forces. It could be tanks, jeeps, food, weapons ... whatever was needed. We used the area around Lakehurst Naval Air Center and McGuire Air Force Base. Lakehurst was known for the giant hangers that held blimps used by the military.

A successful CARP target hit required the navigator to know the winds at every level over the target that would affect the direction of the wind on the dropped cargo. The navigator would calculate the speed of the aircraft, the weight of the cargo, the winds aloft, the size of the chute, and the heading to give the pilot to hold onto the targeted spot of the drop. The pilot would continue at the heading and speed, and would then pop up to the drop altitude within the time given, as calculated by the navigator. The Navigator would tell the Loadmaster when to open the rear cargo door. He would give the Loadmaster the verbal "green light," and the Loadmaster would immediately deploy the chute to drag out the cargo to be parachuted to the ground target.

One day, I drew *Crazy* Ted as the lead pilot for this airdrop training. He did everything I told him to do as the Navigator, until we got close to the drop zone. At that point, Ted began saying, "this doesn't look right. I can tell by my drift that we're off." I assured him that the high winds were adequately calculated, and he needed to hold the heading I gave him to "crab" into the winds.

95

I also told him I had just confirmed with operations that the winds were still as calculated. I gave the signal to climb up to drop altitude, and asked Ted to let me know when we reached back to our level airspeed. I gave the Loadmaster the verbal signal over the intercom to open the rear cargo door, and wait for the green light signal to drop. Each crewmember could hear whatever was said to any crewmember through their earphones. I was about to signal, "green light," when Ted yelled, "Hold Up … Okay, now." The Loadmaster hesitated just enough when Ted yelled, then dropped. That split second hesitation caused us to be past the ground target, and we dropped the jeep right into the middle of a New Jersey traffic circle.

I can just imagine the shock of a jeep crashing onto the grassy traffic circle that commuters were going around. *Crazy* Ted had done it again. He always thought he knew best and the rules did not apply to him, whether in combat or training. I did not get in trouble, because for once, the crew was interviewed after we were on the evening news. They told the truth about Ted overriding the mission calculations by the Navigator (me), which caused us to make the traffic circle drop.

By now, I think one of those movies about active duty servicemen's antics could include *Crazy* Ted. Crews were drawn at random, and eventually, everyone flew with about every other crewmember in our squadron of 230 officers and men. When I think about my own extraordinary experiences with Ted, I wonder how many *Crazy* Ted stories must be out there that I don't even know about; stories that others flying with Ted must have experienced? If taken all together, it probably could make for a very funny movie.

# BICYCLES at CHRISTMAS

*"For your father knoweth what things ye have need of
before ye ask him."* Matthew 6:8

It had been a bad year in real estate. I was broke! I had no savings, no stocks to sell, nothing of value to pawn and no credit cards. I had melted them all on a Pam-greased baking sheet to come off credit. I had absolutely nothing ... no resource from which I could draw upon or borrow. Moreover, it was Christmas, and my daughters wanted bikes for Christmas. My wife and I were troubled that we had no way of providing what our six and eight year old daughters wanted for Christmas. After all, was it such a big thing to ask for ... bikes? However, if you cannot provide them, it becomes huge!

We began to prepare our daughters. We told them how tough the year had been; that they were not going to be able to get bikes this year. Undaunted, they simply said, "Yes we will... we'll ask GOD for them." (Sometimes, when you try to model a life of faith, you can create "monsters".) After tucking them into bed and hearing their sweet prayers asking God for bikes for Christmas, and even thanking God in advance for providing their bikes, my wife and I came down the stairs in shock, depressed, and sullen over our children's positive prayers. We knew what they were praying for to happen was impossible. In desperation, we went downstairs and knelt by the couch across from the Christmas tree. We cried out to God to not disappoint our daughters or allow their faith to be destroyed by tomorrow morning. This was the most depressing, saddest Christmas Eve we had ever spent. Our evening was spent rehearsing the wording of our explanation just right for the next morning when their prayers were not answered, when they would wake up to nothing under the tree. Mostly, we talked about having to defend God for not answering their prayers. We anticipated what theological dancing we were going to have to do around their questions and disappointment.

About 10:00 pm, I received a call from my good friend, Larry Burkett. He said he had just received a call from a man who had a ministry of buying old bikes, painting and fixing them up to give to those who needed them and could not afford them. Larry asked if I knew anyone at this late hour on Christmas Eve that could use a couple of small girls bikes for Christmas. I thought my heart was going to pound out of my chest. I said, "Of course I do... I need them," I told him. I told him how my wife and I had just been praying for that very thing.

He gave me the man's name and phone number to call. The name sounded familiar to me. I called and got directions to his house. As if I had not been humbled enough that year, the reason his name sounded familiar was because he was a man involved with the Christian school where my children attended. He could not believe that WE were the ones needing the bikes. My wife and I served as head of the Parent Teachers Fellowship at our school, and we had been successful in hiding and covering up our financial needs from everyone. I loaded the two girls' bikes into my trunk and headed home. My wife was so excited when I pulled out beautiful yellow and purple bikes. They were reconditioned to look like new.

We put them around the Christmas tree and now could hardly sleep because we were so excited; not just because we actually got bikes, but also because we were let off the hook for all the theological questions about faith, believing God, and answers to prayer that we were NOT going to have to deal with the next morning. Instead, we were rehearsing how we were going to tell them about how faithful God was to answer their prayers.

Sure enough, Cathy and Christy came downstairs early Christmas morning to find their bikes under the tree. They each grabbed one and rode "Purple Cow" and "Yellow Daisy" (as they named them) around and around the cul-de-sac on our street. After they were exhausted and needed a breakfast break, we had the pleasurable opportunity to tell them the story of what had transpired the prior evening after they had prayed and gone to bed, and how their bikes *really were* an answer to their prayers, as well as ours.

Well, those two bikes had more meaning to them because of that miracle provision than if we had been able to afford new bikes without the anguish of praying, believing, and sweating out the answers to our daughter's prayers. What appeared to be the most sad, depressing Christmas Eve ever became the most exciting, extraordinary, positive and enriching Christmas morning experience of our lives. When the pressure is finally off, we still cannot forget that HE said, "... *for your father knoweth what things ye have need of, before ye ask him."* Matthew 6:8.

That is so TRUE. What an extraordinary Christmas.

# EARLY SALVATION ARMY

*"Who can find a virtuous woman? For her price is far above rubies....she worketh willingly with her hands."* Proverbs 31:10-13

In the 1980's, we were invited to a party at a very wealthy investor's home, who had syndicated many properties to individuals for tax shelter investment purposes. He had really capitalized on his fame as an NFL football player before getting into real estate investments. At the time, I was in the same business ... the main differences between us, besides size, and physical stature, was fame, size of investments, and number of clients. When Congress passed the Tax Reform Act of 1986, we both got into trouble on our syndicated properties. However, as the Act caused all property to be instantly undervalued, and the Savings and Loan industry collapsed due to being instantly under-collateralized on their property to loan values, this man was so big that the banks *hired him* to do the workout of his own chapter 11 bankruptcy reorganizations and foreclosures. I was working out of my own living room in my home office. The invitees to this party were all of high financial stature, except for my wife, Bertie, and me. I expect that he invited us because we knew him and his wife from our Sunday school class. It certainly was not because of our financial status.

I could not relate to the ex-NFL "greats" group bragging in one corner of the living room. Nor could I relate to the number of "zeros" in the deals of the businessmen's group and their stories of huge financial successes in the other corner of the room. Therefore, I wandered into the kitchen area where Bertie was with the other wives. Same thing ... only decorating and furniture stories being told there, with again, huge amounts of money talked about.

I wondered how Bertie was handling that. She was not prone to be "snooty" about anything. Even though I invested other people's money for them, it seemed that for my whole life, I was always the poorest person I knew at most functions.

My wife, Bertie, was one of those genuine people to whom money made no difference. Although she came from upper middle class (her father was Vice President of Winn-Dixie, a grocery chain in the South,) she never measured, judged, or befriended anyone based upon economic status. Therefore, I wondered how Bertie was handling all this designer and furniture "period" talk.

"Our entire home is authentic primitive Early American," said one wife. "Jacobean is the period we love and decorate with," said another. Another wife chimed in, "We just couldn't endure anything less than genuine French. In fact, we've made several trips to Europe to buy almost all of our furniture, and had it shipped over here to us." "How about you, Bertie?" someone asked. I thought, "uh oh."

"Early Salvation Army," Bertie replied. *(There were gasps, from all around.)* She continued, explaining that she shopped at the Salvation Army and Goodwill Thrift Stores for used, but well-made furniture. She then further explained that she had taken a wood refinishing class, as well as upholstery classes. She told them that she had reupholstered our living room couch and chairs. She then began to describe how she drove around in nice neighborhoods on trash pick-up days, looking for a furniture "gem", so that one person's "poison" could become her "pleasure." Yes, she had recovered some of those unwanted chairs and other items discarded to curbside, and had personally upholstered them with deeply discounted fabric ... *(There were more gasps.)* Then she related how she had taken sewing lessons and drapery design classes and had always made our drapes for our homes and even clothes for our daughters ... *(even more gasps).* I cannot even begin to tell you how much "stuffy" air she let out of that room.

We did not stay to be the last ones to leave that party, I might add. I can say that it was refreshing to observe someone like Bertie, so sure of herself, so confident and full of self-esteem, that she never thought of trying to impress anyone. Yet later, as my business prospered, she decorated our 11,000 square foot home we built on 32 acres with such class, that everyone wanted to take photos. Even a French magazine came over from Paris to do a photo-shoot for their article on Bertie's French-styled kitchen cabinets on French legs and the hand-painted tile backsplash that she helped design. Oh ... and the pink silk she had backed by paper so it became wallpaper on the wall to match the pink, silk upholstery on the dining room chairs. She certainly had the good taste and class, if the money were there to do it.

What a blessing, to be so gifted and able to step up to the highest level needed for the times and moments, yet be so humble that she took classes, picked up furniture off the street curbs, and "worked with her hands" to do whatever was necessary for the economic times. I definitely would call Bertie a "virtuous woman" according to Proverbs 31, *"She worked willingly with her hands, and her price is far above rubies."* She was an extraordinary woman. Oh, and I do recommend Early Salvation Army when you are starting out married life.

# PEANUTS

*"Giving thanks always for all things unto God."*
Ephesians 5:20

I was broke. I had left my stockbroker's job at Merrill Lynch to start my own company to syndicate apartment building properties. I was determined to be careful with purchases, and only tie up real estate I could "steal" at a low price. In my experience, the profit and value on a property is determined by the purchase price at the time you buy it. To date, I had used up all my reserves. I sold my Merrill Lynch stock and used up those proceeds, and I was broke. I could not even buy a meal. On my last outing to look at a property, I swung by the Farmers Market in South Atlanta (Forest Park), and bought a huge, 50-lb, burlap bag of Georgia peanuts. I had roasted them on a flat baking sheet in the oven, and placed them in a large wooden bowl in the middle of our dining table in the breakfast nook in the kitchen. My wife and I were debating on just how we were going to tell our daughters when they came in from school that those peanuts were ALL we had to eat in the house. We were not looking forward to that disclosure.

Meanwhile, a realtor, (I will call him "Roger"), dropped by with a "deal" in which he thought I would be interested. We knew each other well. The garage door was open, and Roger came through the garage into the kitchen. He sat down at the kitchen table, and began laying out paperwork on an apartment, including plats, deeds, photos and financials. I sat down across from him as Roger began to describe the deal.

After talking about 30 minutes, Roger reached into the wooden bowl of peanuts and pulled out a handful. He cracked them open quickly, one-by-one, and tossed them into his mouth.

Then, he grabbed a second handful and ate them, too. In horror, I watched him grab a third handful. When he saw the look on my face, he said, "Don't worry! I will clean these shells up when I am finished. These are great peanuts ... roasted just perfectly."

I did not know what to say. When he grabbed yet another handful, I blurted out "Roger, you're eating our dinner for tonight." "Yeah, Right," He chuckled ... "Right!" I guess it was a little unbelievable that someone trying to buy an apartment complex was actually broke, and that this was "really" their entire dinner. Honestly, I was so stressed that my mind blocked him out – I was not hearing a thing he said after that. I hurried up the meeting, stacking all the paperwork in a pile, and walking him to the door, telling him that I would go over everything in detail, and get back to him later.

In actuality, when the door closed behind him, I ran to the pantry, opened the large burlap bag of peanuts on the floor, grabbed enough handfuls to cover a baking pan sheet, fired up the oven, and began roasting that night's supper to replace what had been eaten before my daughters arrived home from school. Eventually, we reached a place where we never lacked for food to eat.

This extraordinary occurrence will always be fresh in my memory, and I have never lacked gratitude since then, for even the simplest provision in life. *"Giving thanks always for all things unto God. "* Ephesians 5:20

# BUY OUT

*"And whosoever shall compel thee to go a mile,
go with him two."* Matthew 5:41

The builder was evicting us because I could not pay the rent on the house. Where was I going to go? If I could not pay the rent on this house, where was I going to get the money to pay the rent somewhere else? The problem was not the house. The lack of money was the problem.

I had left Merrill Lynch as a stockbroker, sold my home, sold my stock, and rented this 2-story Colonial Williamsburg on a cul-de-sac. The housing market was soft, and new houses were sitting unsold. I had rented this new home from two builders with an option to buy. I figured I would close a real estate deal before my reserves ran out. Well, it did not happen. Now, I was out of money and could not even pay the rent, much less exercise the option to purchase the house. Each of the two partner builders alternated coming by to collect rent, and each time I had to tell them I did not have it to give. I guess they figured they almost had to ride with me on my hopes because the real estate market had become so bad.

The market soon turned, and as houses began selling again, the pressure toward me to move became greater. They wanted to sell the house, and I was preventing it by occupying it as a renter. I did not blame them, but the housing market was turning up faster than the commercial market, where I was trying to make my living. I just could not pay. It soon became obvious that the older partner was relying upon the younger one, Jimmy, to get me out. Jimmy kept coming by telling us that his partner was getting angry, and wanted us out so they could put the house on the market. They really wanted us to buy. We told Jimmy we were praying every day and working hard, but had just not closed anything.

My wife and I prayed daily, pleading with God to intervene in our situation. We had absolutely no funds to pay to move, or to pay to stay. One day, Jimmy came by the house and told us he felt they should "ride with us," but could not. Time was up. Since they were beginning to sell their new houses again, Jimmy bought out his partner's half interest on the house we were living in. He was now the 100% owner. He said this meant he could ride with us until we could pay to buy the house. What a miracle!

Eventually, we closed a deal, and I was able to pay off all back rent, and show enough income for loan qualification to buy the home, which we did with a zero-down VA Loan. We would never have had that opportunity were it not for the extraordinary miracle of the builder having mercy on us, buying out his partner so he was in total control of the situation, and bless us with the grace of his kindness. Jimmy certainly went the *"extra mile"* with us. God is good. It was an extraordinary experience to get us out of a dire, pressured situation.

# BACKFIRE

*"I was almost in all evil in the midst
of the congregation and assembly."* Proverbs 5:14

I have heard it said... "No good deed goes unpunished." It seemed to be true for me on this one.

There was a table in front of the pulpit in our church, on the lower level, that always had a huge vase of fresh flowers in a beautiful arrangement. Someone in the church always bought the flowers, and they would place a memorial saying, a verse, or a comment in the church bulletin dedicating the arrangement to a person or occasion. The thought was to honor the memory of a deceased family member, or to honor someone living, like a husband or wife, with a kind comment about them or anything else as an appropriate recognition.

I scheduled far in advance with the church secretary to take the Sunday that fell on my wife's birthday that year, to honor her. It was to be a complete surprise for her when she sat down in the pew, opened her Sunday service bulletin, and read the kind comment I said about her to honor her. The bulletin was to say:

HAPPY BIRTHDAY, BERTIE

From Your Loving Husband, Dean

Proverbs 31:10

Proverbs 31:10 says, *"Who can find a virtuous woman? For her price is far above rubies."* Well, they got the verse "10" correct, but the chapter number was incorrect. It was not even close. They printed Proverbs 7:10, by mistake. The bulletin read:

"The flowers today are from Dean Webb in honor
of his wife, Bertie's, Birthday today."
Proverbs 7:10

Well, imagine all the looks as people looked up Proverbs 7:10 and found that it said, *"And, behold, there met him a woman with the attitude of a harlot, and subtle of heart."*

Bertie was mad, embarrassed and humiliated, as all the church "eyes" glared at her after they read the verse, and wondered just what was up with our relationship. What a backfire of a good deed and an attempt at a surprise. This attempted good deed was certainly punished.

Bertie forgave and got over it. Eventually, she even laughed about it. It was more difficult for me! The church secretary's "typo" had caused an extraordinary embarrassment, as well as destroyed what should have been a wonderful, loving surprise for her.

# THE LAND

*"Prepare thy work without, and make it fit for thyself in the field; and afterwards build thine house."* Proverbs 24:27

It is not that our 4-bedroom home on a cul-de-sac was not private. Because of the pie-shaped lots, we could not even see a neighbor's house to either side from our back porch (great privacy for our hot tub). In fact, there was no one behind us either because our lot backed up to hundreds of vacant acres adjacent to Stone Mountain State Park, east of Atlanta. I do not think you could live on a half-acre lot in a major city and be more surrounded by land, yet be so private.

However, my youngest daughter, Christy, wanted a horse, which would take land to keep. When we bought her first horse, she was in grade school, so we had to pay monthly to pasture-board her horse on another farm property near us. My wife and I decided to pray for property we could own on which to keep her horse. We decided to be very specific in our list of property requirements that we were going to pray for, so we would *know* that it was an answer to our prayers when we found it. We listed:

- Acreage that included pasture not far from our current home
- Near Atlanta off a major highway into Atlanta
- Water on it (lake or river)
- Existing living structure on the property

We prayed, and then began to drive around and look. We read the ads for property in the paper every weekend. We prayed, read, and drove around looking for "For Sale" signs on land. We drove in ever-increasing circles from our current house. After 2 years, we had covered the ground so far away from our current location, and we were so far outside Atlanta that we would not even want it if we found it. We let it rest and even stopped looking.

After 3 years, we began looking again, while praying, reading ads, and driving in ever-increasing circles away from our house, but to no avail. For 5 years, we had been praying our criteria list and looking to no avail! It looked like we had created a fantasy set of criteria... unrealistic... non-existent.

Suddenly, unexpectedly, my attorney called me and asked if I was still looking for land for our horse? I said, "Yes." He said he and his partner found 200 acres they were going to develop but needed some up-front cash to develop the county road into the property. He said if I had the money, I could pick out whatever acreage I wanted, pay cash for it, and then they would use that up-front money to do the road, survey the lots, and begin development of the property. I agreed to look at it.

When he told me the location, I said "No way! That is just 2-3 miles from my house, and I have been down every road around me." I knew right where he was talking about, because I had been down that dirt road many times. However, I knew of no property for sale there. He said it was hidden from the road by undergrowth and overgrown hedges, and it could not be seen from the dirt road. He also said it was entangled in a divorce settlement. It was just now available for sale in order to settle the divorce-required division of assets. Besides the close proximity, it also had frontage on a river. We had prayed for water as another part of our conditions. He described in detail where the entry to the property was.

Once again, I went off Highway 78 (Stone Mountain Expressway) the equivalent of about 3 city blocks, went down to the lowest part of the road and looked to the right. I could see it ... an old metal farm gate hidden behind unkempt hedges, foliage and drooping tree limbs. I unlocked and pushed the gate open, then drove my car through.

WOW! The break-through was to a vista of open rolling hills of pasture, with horses grazing all over the property. It was beautiful. It was a miracle that this property was hidden right under my nose. Every facet of the condition we wanted: close by; major highway; pastures; water (a couple of thousand feet of frontage on the Yellow River); and, an existing structure ... a log cabin built in 1869, just a dozen feet away from the Yellow River rapids.

When God answers prayer, He does it right. In God's timing, He revealed everything I wanted that was hidden and preserved right under my nose. It was more beautiful than I had been imagining. I picked out the land I wanted and had it surveyed. It had some forest, some pasture, and 905 feet of frontage on the River, plus, the 1869 log cabin. I closed on it quickly, before anyone could change their mind.

The cabin is one of the most extraordinary structures I have ever seen, and the property it sits on is extraordinary as well. Everyone remarks about its beauty, closeness to the river rapids, serenity and peacefulness. To think that all the time it was so close to us, and we did not even know it. God is so awesome! We simply realized we were praying and unknowingly waiting on His timing for the property to become available. Meanwhile, the property was hidden from view, right under our noses, close to us.

# FAMILY REUNIONS

*"And thy seed shall be as the dust of the earth, and thou shalt spread abroad to the West, and to the East, and to the North, and to the South: and in thee and in thy seed shall all the families of the earth be blessed."* Genesis 28:14

Every year, our family got together for 1-2 weeks either in the summer, or from Christmas to New Years ... sometimes both ... a week each. We had 28-35 family members show up, including children. They came from Georgia, Oklahoma, Texas, California, and Chicago ... all over the map. I had a 32-acre property with our 11,000 square foot home, plus our cabin that slept eight. Often, my sister, Ruth, and her husband, Bill, would also host the reunion in their home in Tulsa. Whatever the accommodations, we were packed like sardines because there were so many of us, but we loved it.

My sister, Ruth, would scout out locations for us to meet, too. For two separate years, we rented the town of Dry Gulch, Oklahoma, during the week of Christmas through New Years. Dry Gulch was an authentic western town that was a summer camp for children and used as a set for Christian Western movies. Since there were no camping activities during the holidays, we could rent the entire town from Christmas to New Years. In the two block-long, western town, all stores, jail, saloon, dry goods store, and barbershop had rooms for sleeping built above them on the second floor. The accommodations ranged from open dorms to private rooms and apartments. Some even had suites with living room areas and kitchens. The large meeting hall at the end of the town street had a large rock fireplace at one end and was actually a dining hall with a commercial sized kitchen for feeding 200 campers at the summer camps. The first year we rented the town, we were able to hire the cook who worked there to cook for us during our entire stay. The second year, he took the holiday off, and we drew straws for the days each of the ten couples would be responsible for cooking all the meals for everyone. That way, no one gave up more than one day for cooking leaving all the other days as free time.

Another Christmas, we rented a huge doctor's home with ten bedrooms on a thousand foot tall plateau near Little Rock, Arkansas. We drew numbers for the days we were responsible for cooking, leaving everyone free every day, except for their one day to cook meals. We chose teams and had paint ball wars in the woods all day until we were exhausted, and it was time for dinner. We would shower for dinner and have wonderful conversations around the tables. After dinner, as we always did each day of each reunion, we all met in the huge lodge-type living room and did our traditional format.

First, we went around the room and each person took five minutes to update everyone on their life over the last year since we were last together. At the end of everyone's updates, we gave our most urgent prayer request. We always nominated a "scribe" for that reunion to write down the current needs and prayer requests. That request time usually took up to three hours.

The Scribe then read the prayer request from the previous reunions and each person announced the status of that situation. They either told how the prayer was answered, or said that we needed to continue praying for that need. If we had time and it was not too late, we would begin our family prayer meeting. Usually, we always began our prayers with the youngest child and worked up in age through the singles and then the couples.

The format was the same each time. We placed a chair in the middle of the family circle in the room. They expressed their prayer request (or parent did it if a very small child). We gathered around the person in the chair, laid hands on them, and prayed as each one felt led, for that person's request. Then, we took the next one, until we prayed for each one. It usually took a full week of nights to complete the round of praying for everyone. Of course, the designated scribe recorded those prayer requests to be able to remind the group of them at the next reunion.

One year we went to Ann, my other sister's home in California. We took a break on New Year's Eve and camped out in their RV on Colorado Boulevard the night before the Rose Bowl Parade. We took turns sleeping on the available beds for an hour each, and then walked the Colorado Boulevard parade route, stopping in each game store. My brother, Jerry, felt it was necessary and his duty to achieve the highest score on every single electronic game or pinball machine, so he could leave his initials "JLW" in lights on the game beside his record scores. The whole scene was bizarre to me. People brought old couches to set on the curb facing the street so they had a front row view of tomorrows elaborate floats. The street was lined with people spending the night on couches that they did not intend to remove at the completion of the Parade of Roses.

I've had people express to me how the most stressful time of the year for them was being with their relatives at their annual family picnic, reunion, or other get together. I have had numerous people over the years tell me how much they even dreaded their annual family picnic and could not wait to exit the occasion after a couple of hours. I simply cannot relate to that. Whether our time to leave occurred after one week, or two, it was a tearful departure for all. We were all energized and strengthened by playing together and praying together. We all looked forward to our annual reunion, wherever it was, and we were all so much better for them happening. We wept when each family member had to leave, starting with the earliest departure. Getting together as a large family from all over the U.S. was always an extraordinary experience and the highlight of our year. I have yet to find another family that does reunions like ours.

# ANNUAL FAMILY INVENTORY

*"Train up a child in the way he should go: and when he is old, he will not depart from it."* Prov. 22:6

For 14 years, I raised my daughters under the ministry of Dr. Charles Stanley in Atlanta, Georgia. I do not know what I would have done without his ministry directed toward fathers.

For example, he instructed the Fathers to take their family away each January for a full day. The outing could be to a hotel, resort, state park; whatever you could afford. The only conditions were that you had to be able to get alone, with no distractions. Each family member had to fill out an Inventory on family members, including themselves. Each person had to set goals for themselves, as well as each of the other family members. Those goals were in the areas of:

- Social and Friendships
- Spiritual – Devotional and Prayer
- Giving Goals (financial)
- Joint Family Goals
- Health (exercise, weight, etc.)

In addition, you had to complete these statements for each family member:

- Things you *do* that I wish you *would stop doing*
- Things you *do* that I like, and wish you would *continue doing*
- Things you *don't do* that I wish you *would do*
- Things you *don't do* that I hope you *never start doing*

Let me tell you … by the time you get one of these back from each family member, especially your children, I can assure you that you will have "blind spots" pointed out that need working on that you did not know existed. In addition, the fact that they are written down creates a stronger possibility that they will be accomplished. Then, you pray over all the sheets, and ask God to help you to accomplish them, both as a family and individually.

An example of how powerful this exercise was occurred when my wife, my two daughters and I flew to a family reunion in St. Charles, Missouri, between Christmas and New Years. One night, everyone except us had something to do. I borrowed my brother's car and we went to a restaurant to set the annual goals. We ended up in the lounge, since no one was at the bar, where we wrote down annual goals for everyone, exchanged them, discussed them, and then prayed over them. We got back into the car, folded up the goal sheets and placed them in the glove compartment. We drove back to my sister's house and forgot about them.

Six or seven years later, my brother traded that car in. As he cleaned out all his paperwork, he discovered our goal sheets in the glove compartment and sent them to us. Here is the powerful thing: Even though we failed to take them with us and never thought about them again, every family member accomplished every goal that we set years before on the sheets.

By taking it seriously, writing down goals, discussing them for clarity, praying over them, and then asking God for help to accomplish them, we had subconsciously brought all of them to pass with God's help. We never consciously thought about them again, yet we accomplished everything successfully. What an extraordinary way for a family to operate. Thank you, Dr. Stanley, for your wisdom and guidance. This became an annual way of life for us.

# LOST BIBLE IN BERMUDA

*"And all things, whatsoever ye shall ask in prayer
believing, ye shall receive."* Matthew 21:22

My wife and I had been on such a pleasant trip ... our first trip to the island of Bermuda. For the first time, we experienced the pink sandy beaches of Bermuda, the police officers directing traffic in their Bermuda shorts uniforms, and everyone driving on the "wrong side" of concrete streets made of seashells instead of gravel. The round, floating glass bottom and topped pool in the harbor of the Sonesta Beach Hotel, the Hallelujah Chorus done by an all steel drum band, and pastel houses ... it was all just a fairy land of British accents and sensory overload. However, unpacking upon returning home, I could not find my Bible. Where was my Bible?

I took my Bible everywhere I went. I was immersing myself in scripture to build myself up spiritually as much as possible. My Bible was not just *any* Bible. I had yellow highlights, underlined scriptures, notes in the margins, and my other very personalized endearments to enable study and reference. It was very used. In fact, it had disintegrated, and I had to send it off for rebinding so I could continue to use it.

We turned everything inside out ... all the pieces of luggage and carry-on bags, but no Bible. I called back to the hotel, airport, and cabs we rode in, but no one claimed to have seen it.

Using the only asset I could use at this point, I began to pray. I would remind God on a daily basis that I believed in prayer to have my Bible returned. At this point, however, it would take a miracle. I prayed daily for three months for the return of my Bible. Mentally and logically, you know this is an impossible request. However, in faith, you just do not stop asking. My mother came to visit during this time, and she was so upset when she heard me pacing back and forth upstairs, holding my other Bible in my hand above my head, shouting out verses, and reminding God of His Words. I believed He would get my favorite Bible returned. When challenged by my mother, I told her I was not disrespecting God. On the contrary, I wanted HIM to know that I believed HIS Word; asking in prayer, *believing* that I would receive my Bible back, no matter how big a miracle it took.

After four months of daily prayer, I received a letter in a thin, airmail stationery envelope with a lot of postage on it, *from Bermuda!* In it, a chambermaid told of cleaning up a room in her hotel, *which was at the other end of the Island from where we had stayed*. A couple packing their bags had thrown the Bible down on the bed, saying they did not know how that Bible got into in their luggage. "It must have fallen out of a bag at the airport, and they just placed it back in the wrong bag," they said.

She picked it up. She could tell it was well worn and very used. She figured it was important to me and decided to write to the name and address in the front of the Bible. I quickly wrote a letter back, with cash for postage and a reward for her efforts. Within three weeks, I had my favorite Bible back for my daily devotions and study.

You could say that it was a mere "coincidence" that everything happened the way it did. However, having lived through the months of hopelessness, struggling in daily prayer and requests and impassioned pleas to God, people telling me that I should just "consider it lost," and others saying my hopes were a lost cause, I know that it was a miracle and an answer to prayer. Moreover, it did remind me that He said, *"... whatsoever ye shall ask in prayer, believing, ye shall receive."* Matthew 21:22.

This was truly an extraordinary occurrence ... that a chambermaid in a hotel on the opposite end of the Island of where we stayed was there in the room when guests said it wasn't theirs and threw my Bible down on the bed as they were about to check out. Then, the chambermaid took the time and personal expense to write a letter and send it to me via airmail. What an extraordinary answer to my prayers!

# STEAM BATH IN THE SAN ANDREAS FAULT

*"A time to be born and a time to die."* Ecclesiastes 3:2

It was eerie. The groans were coming from the bowels of the earth through a crack in the rock; the same crack in the rock that was belching forth steam. I was scared to be there. We had taken the hotel elevator down some distance, and we were in the bottom of the Arrowhead Springs Hotel in California. We were sitting on a rock in a cavern taking a steam bath beside a crack in the rocks that was belching forth steam and groaning sounds from the San Andreas Fault.

I had accompanied my friend, Larry Burkett, to the Campus Crusade meeting at Arrowhead Springs Hotel in California, where he was to speak. Larry insisted that I join him in the "steam room" before dinner. After we got down there, Larry informed me that source of the steam in the "steam room" was from the Saint Andreas Fault. *"You've got to be kidding me,"* I said.

Conrad Hilton had once owned the Arrowhead Springs Hotel, and I figured that there was nothing to fear. If it had been dangerous, would he have purchased it? Additionally, if dangerous, why would it have become such a Hollywood "place to be?" After all, Judy Garland, Al Jolson, and Rudy Vallee were among those featured at the all-star grand opening in 1939, and, Elizabeth Taylor honeymooned with Nicky Hilton on the sixth floor.

We put on swim trunks, wrapped in large towels, and took the elevator down to the basement floor where the steam room was located. I never really thought about how it would feel to be so close to the fault. Larry was very confident and matter-of-fact about it. There was no way I could let Larry see my fear. However, since I now knew the hot springs were due to the proximity of the San Andreas Fault, I sat there imagining where I would run if the earth started shaking. There was nowhere to run. It felt like we were almost down *in* it. How much closer could we get? We were surrounded by a cavern of huge rocks in the basement of a huge hotel. If the ground opened up, we certainly would have been buried alive under the crushing weight of the six-story hotel. Every minute down there felt like fifteen minutes. Suddenly, I had absolutely no interest in being down there. I left Larry alone and took the elevator back up to my room.

When we discussed my sudden exit later, Larry said I would not "go" before God wanted me to go, so I was safe in the palm of His hand. Even so, taking a steam bath with steam coming from a fissure so close above the San Andreas Fault was not for me. Why tempt fate? I did not want to go before my time. However, just in case it *was* my time to go that day, I sure did not want to go that way. Larry was OK that it was not going to be his time to go. As it turned out, he was correct. Overall, as Larry reminded me, in Ecclesiastes 3:2 it says that there is "*... a time to be born and a time to die.*" I do have to say that although scary, it was an extraordinary experience and memory for me.

# TIMING

*"To everything there is a season and a time
to every purpose under the heaven."* Ecclesiastes 3:1

In my prayer time in the morning, I felt so strongly that I should give Larry Burkett's ministry, Christian Financial Concepts, Inc., a $15,000 donation. It was perfect timing because we had a Board of Directors meeting coming up, and I was on the Board. At a break, I would simply hand the check to him.

At the Board meeting, Larry told how the ministry needed $30,000 immediately for some building project, and I thought, "Wow, I have half of that in a check in my pocket now." I was about to speak up when several Board members around the table spoke and said how much they could give. Between all of them, in a matter of moments, the amount given was determined to be the total of the $30,000 needed. They did not even need my $15,000, so I was wondering why I felt so clearly that God told me to do that?

Several times during the day's meeting and breaks, I started to give the check to Larry anyway, but I just could not; and I did not know why. I left that day's board meeting with the $15,000 check in my pocket, saying nothing to anyone about it. I thought that was strange. The next morning, in prayer, I felt God was telling me to *"wait."* That happened several days in a row.

Finally, one morning in prayer, I felt God was saying, *"Now!"* I grabbed the check, put it in my pocket, and headed over to Norcross, Georgia, to Larry's office. When I got there, the receptionist said to go on back to Larry's building out back. (The offices were in five small, converted outbuildings that used to be part of a farm, and Larry's office was in the back). When I opened the door to Larry's office, I felt bad, because I interrupted him; he was on his knees in prayer. I tried to back out, quietly and apologetically, but Larry told me he was finished praying, and to *"come on in."* He said, "I want you to pray with me about something. I just got word that we need $15,000 to print our next financial workbook. We just raised $30,000 a couple of weeks ago from the Board." Larry continued, "It is hard to get people to give to materials. They will readily give to building projects, but are usually more reluctant to give to on-going operational costs or printing. And, the needs have come so close together." I told Larry I did not need to pray with him, because I had already prayed, and God had spoken to me and told me to bring this, pulling the two-week-old, $15,000 check out of my pocket and handing it to him. He was so happy. Then he noticed the older date on the check and asked about it.

I told him how I had felt led to write the check weeks earlier, but had just not felt it was time to give it to him. Now, I knew why. Ecclesiastes 3:1 says, *"There is a time to every purpose under the heaven."*

The timing for obedience was now, for the exact time he was praying for the need that we did not even know existed when I wrote the check. Nothing is more exciting than obedience to the inner voice of God, and His timing is perfect. Personally, I think people miss a lot of "life" by not living close to God's voice in their Spirit. They miss experiencing extraordinary events like this.

# LARRY BURKETT: "PULL the PLUG"

*"But let your communication be, Yea, Yea; Nay, Nay: for whatsoever is more than these, cometh of evil."* Matthew 6:37

I was most fortunate when Larry's widow, Judy, asked me to be the final speaker and give a tribute to Larry before the pastor spoke at Larry Burkett's memorial service on July 11, 2003. Larry passed away on July 4, 2003, and the memorial service was at the Church of the Apostles in Atlanta. The incident I told about Larry at his memorial service was in newspapers all over the country; copies of my talk were in newspapers, sent to me from as far away as California.

I always loved to be around Larry because he was the same behind closed doors as he was in public. What you saw, was what you got. He did not just "talk the talk" but he "walked the walk." In my experience, that was rare around people in ministry. I once asked Larry how he could always be so relaxed about donations coming in to support the ministry when he did not do fundraising. He said, "It's easy because it's not *my* ministry. It's *God's* ministry, and He has to fund it."

The incident I related at his memorial service was when I found out that was true for Larry. He called me one day in December 1983, after he had moved the ministry headquarters from Norcross, Georgia, to Dahlonega, Georgia, and the donations had dropped dramatically. He told me he was going to announce that he was shutting down the ministry. Of course, I strongly protested. God had called him to start that ministry, and so many lives were affected positively by its message. Larry acknowledged that it would be so sad to stop the ministry. However, he also reminded me that he told God he was willing to do it, but God was going to have to finance it.

Of course, the Board also argued, prayed and begged, but Larry was firm on his commitment to shut down for lack of finances and support. I thought, *"WOW - this guy really does believe it is not 'his' ministry."*

A couple of days later, Larry called me and said a miracle had happened. While he was preparing to address the staff upon their return from lunch about terminating their employment, a U.S. postal truck pulled up with duffle bags full of mail. It seems a manager at the post office in Norcross, Georgia, noticed an enormous accumulation of mail in the "dead letter" file area. These huge duffle bags were full of mail addressed to the same entity, Christian Financial Concepts, Inc. It seems that when the ministry moved from Norcross to Dahlonega, someone had messed up on the mail forwarding instructions, and the duffle bags that stacked up contained over four month's worth of mail. They were now delivering the mail to the mountains of Dahlonega. When the staff returned from lunch, instead of being told they were being let go, they all began opening mail and the recording of those letters that had contributions in them. After days of opening mail, there was over four month's worth of support donated within those envelopes. In addition, since most non-profits receive about a third of their annual contributions in the last quarter due to the typical surge in year-end giving, there was a surplus of funds to jump-start the budget for the next year.

That was a defining moment for me. I was able to experience, firsthand and up close, the faith and trust Larry Burkett had in God. In my lifetime, I have heard many people *say* that they "trust God."

However, when the pressure is on, they do not … not really. When the pressure was on, Larry really did. That is rare, today. Matthew 6:37 says, *"But let your communication be, Yea, Yea; Nay, Nay: for whatsoever is more than those cometh of evil."*

I was fortunate enough to be close to Larry's ministry and see his total trust in God to provide. It resulted in my being personally aware of this extraordinary miracle of God's timing for provision. How wonderful is that?

# OBEDIENCE on $5,000

*"To obey is better than sacrifice."* I Samuel 15:22

During my morning devotions, in my mind I kept seeing an image of a football player who spoke at the Pro Athletes Outreach (PAO) Conference. I was on the Board of Directors for PAO, which provided three retreats per year for pro athletes. Sometimes, one of the Christian former athletes spoke. Dallas Cowboys player, Dave Simmons, was one of those. When he spoke, he said he retired from football to start a family ministry in Arkansas and a children's summer camp ministry in Mississippi. At the time, I did not think much about it.

However, when I returned home, while I was in prayer morning after morning, Dave's face would come into my mind with the thought to send his ministry $5,000. WOW! First, why would an ex-professional football player need money? I did not even know his ministry, or even remember where it was located. I thought, "Can this truly be God speaking to me?"

I called the PAO office in Seattle, and I got Dave's phone number. They told me he was currently in Hattiesburg, Mississippi, where he was opening a summer camp for underprivileged kids.

I called the number given to me, and it rang and rang. Even though it was an hour earlier there than where I was in Atlanta, I was beginning to wonder if they had given me a wrong number. I knew they should be in the office because I had waited to call Seattle until I thought the PAO office would be open. Seattle was three time zones earlier than Atlanta. Since no person or answering machine picked up in Mississippi, I just let it ring.

Finally, a man answered the phone. I announced that I was calling from Atlanta to speak with Dave Simmons. "This is Dave," he answered. I told Dave my name, and that I had heard him speak at the last PAO conference. I apologized that I did not remember what he said about his ministry exactly or even where he was. I explained I had obtained this phone number from the PAO office. I further explained that every time I got on my knees to pray in my morning devotions, his face kept popping into my mind with the prompting from God to send him $5,000, but I did not know why.

"Are you kidding me?" He said. "Are you serious?" I said I would not go through all this trouble if I were not serious. I just could not shake God's prompting to send him $5,000. Dave let out a cheer, and said, "I'm going to put you on speaker phone with my staff, and I want you to say again what you just told me." A few seconds later, I was on a speakerphone and Dave said, "Go ahead… tell them what you just told me." I did, and then I heard multiple people in the room shouting praises of "Thank you, God."

Dave took the phone back and said, "You see, our entire staff has been gathered in our conference room praying for funds. We committed to never borrow money to help these kids at this camp. We were praying because it is time to open the summer camp, and we were in a dilemma because we were short $5,000. Not only is this a miracle, but the timing is incredible … right at the time we were gathered to pray. Thank you for your obedience to the prompting from God," Dave said.

That experience taught me that I do not have to know whom, why, or what the details are. If I am sure I have heard from God, just do it. To obey is better than sacrifice. Trusting in the still, small voice of God in my prayer time allowed me to experience this extraordinary event in timing, the correct amount, and an extraordinary answer to precise prayers of both giver and recipient in need. My obedience to God's voice was a real faith-builder to me, as well as to all of those praying staff members in Mississippi.

# 2 QUARTERS

At age 10, my daughter, Catherine, taped 2 quarters to a 3 x 5 card with a note written on the card, and sent it to two lady missionaries we supported in the Sudan in Africa. If the two missionaries had not possessed a U.S. address for receiving their support and mailings, the postage to the Sudan in Africa for the weight would have cost more than Catherine's 50-cent gift. At that time in history, you had to airmail to Africa in those thin, lightweight, onionskin envelopes. The mailing would have been quite expensive.

That 50-cent gift was a sacrifice to Catherine because it represented an hour of babysitting work. Even though she was in demand because of her good work ethic and personality, those jobs came scarcely to most at her young age; and usually only in a maximum of 2-3 hour segments at a time. Therefore, her gift, no matter how small to the overall mission expenses of those two missionaries in the Sudan, was a sacrificial gift representing part of a whole evening of babysitting for her.

Catherine was motivated to give sacrificially (at least sacrificially for her ability to give) because the two missionaries, Mary Beam & Betty Cridland, had told us of successfully saving two twin boys from death in the tribe in the Sudan where they were missionaries. According to the tribal custom and superstition, twins were a curse. Therefore, it was the custom of that tribe to immediately bury all newborn twins alive and leave until dead. The first member of that tribe to convert to Christianity, who asked to be renamed "Paul," had those twin boys. Because of his conversion, he no longer saw the birth of twins as a curse, but a blessing. He let them live. He endured the wrath of his tribe and had to protect himself, his wife, and his two twin boys from being killed. After a visit to the United States, his twin boys, Bullis and Banooni, were renamed "Billy Graham" and "Cliff Barrows." As a family, we committed to pray for and support these two boys through college, and my daughter's gift was a part of that commitment.

We give because we love to; because the need is there; because we are admonished in scripture to do so; and, because we want to help to the degree we are able to help. In fact, the Bible teaches the principal of "sowing and reaping." We give and somehow we reap back into our lives more, for even more sowing into others. Moreover, sometimes we reap back more than we sow, for even more expanded giving.

I do believe that the sowing and reaping principal probably does not work if you are giving *solely* expecting an exact return or multiple returns on your giving. It just is not that directly correlated. It is a mixed blend of motives; heart, attitude, and faith that needs time to produce results and reap a harvest. I just know from experience that you reap more than you sow, later than you sow, and sometimes in a format of goodness that you never expected or even dreamed to receive. The two quarters were like that. This gift to the missionaries from my young daughter resulted in my receiving an incredible meeting and job offer from someone I would have never met on my own.

The founder of Tropicana orange juice, Mr. Anthony Rossi, lived in the Bradenton area of the Gulf Coast of Florida. As it so happened, he was a supporter of these same two missionaries in the Sudan in Africa as well. When they received the two quarters, they told Mr. Rossi about that humble gift of 50-cents they had received from my 10-year old daughter's precious gift of babysitting time. Apparently, he never forgot about that.

Sometime later in 1978, he sold his company, Tropicana Orange Juice, to Beatrice Foods for a reported $450 million. He remembered that gift. He remembered that the missionaries had told him that I, her father, was in the investment business. He asked them, "How can I get in touch with the father of that daughter who gave the two quarters?" He told them he wanted to consider entrusting the management of his money to someone who taught his children to give like that. Therefore, they asked me to come to Bradenton, Florida, to meet with him and to bring my family. Mr. Rossi put us up in his large guest home with a 12-car garage out on a point surrounded by 270-degrees of water views and overlooking the Sunshine Skyway Bridge. It was beautiful.

The home alarm went off when we entered the home using the door key we were furnished. We panicked and called the missionaries for the security code. They said to try Mr. Rossi's birthdate, which they gave us. We tried it, but it did not work. Next, they gave us another set of numbers representing the date Mr. Rossi became a Christian. That worked, and the alarm turned off. That figures … the date Mr. Rossi became a Christian was the most important milestone of his life to him after coming to the United States from Sicily.

Mr. Rossi was the brightest mind I had ever met. He had numerous inventions to assist him in the orange juice business. He said his ideas came from God, and they should not be patented so that they could remain in the public domain for all to use. He said he felt he should not profit personally from those inventions since they were all God-given ideas. What pure motives. He came from Sicily; the place that history says produces most of the Italian mobsters. This guy was the furthest from that.

When Anthony Rossi came to New York and became a Christian, his life, attitudes and motives were transformed. He said he became a Christian when Jesus appeared to him in the New York Library. He had checked out a book the librarian selected for him when he asked her how he could know more about this "Jesus" he kept hearing about. He gave his life to Christ. Upon his salvation, he became a giver. He traveled back to Sicily once a year and helped build a church and a mission. He built a subdivision of hundreds of homes in Bradenton, Florida, called Missionary Village. He gave these homes to missionaries when they returned from the mission fields of the world and had no place to go, no retirement, or had never accumulated anything for their later years. They had given their all on the mission field in unselfish service to others, and Mr. Rossi wanted to take care of them. He even had meals prepared and delivered … a hot meal to each resident in each home once a day to be sure they got at least one, nutritious, hot meal per day.

He paid to have the Bible read and recorded on cassette in the native tongue of Sudan tribes. He then paid to airdrop tape recorders and cassettes into the tribal area of the Sudan in Africa. The recorders were powered by a small crank rather than needing batteries. The cassette tapes recorded the spoken Bible in the native language of those various tribes so they could hear the Bible in their own language. One of his "ideas" (inventions) had governors put on the cranking mechanism so that no matter how fast or slow the natives cranked the airdropped tape recorder, they

140

would hear the Bible in their language at the same speed as spoken and recorded.

This man and his generous heart blew me away. I would have loved to be around this man for an extended period and absorb some of his loving generosity. Any business offer he said he would consider making to me to manage his money would include the requirement for us to move to Bradenton, Florida. Unfortunately, I was on the hook for millions of dollars of syndicated apartment properties, which I personally managed from Atlanta. I told him I simply could not consider any offer, which required moving out of Georgia.

It did not matter... the simple act of 2-quarters taped to a card by a little girl had opened up a door for me to spend time with a genius of industry that I would have otherwise never even had the chance to meet. The simple act of actually meeting this man in person that I had read about as a stockbroker with Merrill Lynch and had seen in the news in the Wall Street Journal, was a huge gift to me. I was encouraged simply to have his consideration for managing his fortune. I reaped an opportunity and life experience worth far more than the gift of 2-quarters, for sure! That extraordinary experience was one of the most exciting memories of my life. You just cannot out-give God!

# WITTY INVENTIONS

*"I, wisdom, dwell with prudence, and find out knowledge of witty inventions."* Proverbs 8:12

There is a table with a 4-foot wide huge roll of thick brown wrapping paper on rollers on the back of a waist-high table in the CEO's office. The paper was there to be pulled, ripped off, and laid down on the table to draw and write out sudden ideas and flashes of genius for inventions. Really? Does anyone ever have so many ideas requiring that quantity and availability of paper to capture and memorialize them before the creative "flash" of genius evaporates?

I was in the second story office of the Founder and CEO of Tropicana orange juice company in Bradenton, Florida. Mr. Anthony Rossi was telling me that he never filed for a patent on any of his ideas because he believed that his inventive ideas came from God, and so they should be in the public domain. I came from Atlanta to meet Mr. Rossi upon his invitation. He wanted someone to manage money he would be receiving from his pending sale of Tropicana to Beatrice Foods ... about $450 Million.

The introduction came through two missionaries that, unknown to either of us, we both happen to support. He found out about me through the missionaries describing a fifty-cent gift to them from one of my daughters, consisting of two quarters taped to a 3 x 5-index card. (See chapter, "2 Quarters")

As I toured his factory, I was amazed at the frozen storage warehouse where thousands of fresh, flash-frozen, huge Tropicana orange juice cubes were sitting on racks, awaiting transport to packaging before shipment to stores and restaurants. The flash-

143

pasteurization concept, invented in 1954, rapidly raised the temperature of juice for a short time to preserve its taste. Then, the bottled juice was shipped as finished goods in refrigerated boxcars. For the first time, consumers could have the fresh taste of pure, not-from-concentrate juice in ready-to-serve chilled packages. This revolutionized the fresh taste of orange juice. Because he never patented his ideas, they were free to be used by others, including his competitors.

As I toured, I was amazed at the "formula" he had created for the cardboard boxes that were made for shipping the bottles of orange juice. After shipment to their destination, they were collected and ground up for cattle feed. When they made the boxes, they actually had nutrients and fiber added into them so they would be consumable as feed … no waste!

Another invention was a claw-like, padded extension on a tractor that could grip the base of an orange tree (like pliers) and shake it until the fruit dropped for quick harvest. Its design would not damage the tree or roots. This allowed them to harvest the oranges so much quicker than individual picking of oranges. They were transported to the processing plant while the oranges were fresh from harvesting.

Yet another invention idea was the creation of a long ramp with a hydraulic cylinder lift beneath it. The truck, full of oranges, would pull up on the ramp, chain its front axle down and the entire platform underneath the truck would lift up. Tilting the oranges toward the back of the long truck bed, the back swivel tailgate would then tilt open at the bottom of the truck bed, and the entire load of fresh oranges would drop out the bottom of the bed onto a conveyor belt running into the grading and packing warehouse.

This allowed the truckload of fresh oranges to be unloaded almost immediately, saving hours of wait time between unloading and processing the juice, thus making a juice that is much fresher from the tree to factory.

Orange peels essence is extracted and sold to perfume manufacturers. When the oil embargo of 1973-74 occurred, Mr. Rossi created an extract from orange peels. When processed and added to the fuel, this extract allowed his trucks to be running the highways when competitors could not get fuel, could not afford fuel, or could not get enough of it to continue business. His mind was amazing.

The noon, lunch-break whistle sounded at the plant. Everyone stopped work to walk to the dining area at one end of the warehouse next to Mr. Rossi's office. The alley between the buildings was hundreds of feet long. Looking down from this second floor vantage point, Mr. Rossi noticed everyone was walking the entire length of the building alley, turning into the end opening, and then walking the entire length of the warehouse back to the end containing the dining area. Suddenly, Mr. Rossi jumped up, raced down the metal fire escape steps outside his office door, grabbed a hardhat, jumped onto a forklift, powered it up, turned it toward the brick wall, and rammed the forklift through the wall. He then told a shocked Foreman standing nearby in Mr. Rossi's strong Sicilian accent, "Get someone to square that hole up into a door opening so the men would not have to waste their time walking so far around the building to get to the lunchroom." Mr. Rossi raced back up the outside stairs to the second floor, opened his office door, sat down and continued his conversation with me in a normal tone of voice, as if what he just impetuously did was "normal." Actually, to him, as a man of action, it was normal.

He then invited me to his home for some of his country's home-style Sicilian pizza. He also freshly ground and brewed coffee he took from a 50 lb burlap bag of coffee beans from Columbia. I could not believe how cordial and hospitable this multi-millionaire was to me.

While he was making pizza, I noticed through the walls of glass that the back of his home was on the water. His home was in the shape of a large "U" with the opening facing the water. There were multiple steps around the three sides of the "U" into the water, allowing him to walk down steps to the salt water level and swim, regardless of how low or how high the tide. There were steps down to whatever the bay's water level was, so Mr. Rossi could enjoy swimming in salt water at any time without leaving the comfort of his home. The opening of the "U" was closed with wire under the water to keep the fish out of the natural, 3-sided, salt-water pool. This was just another example of his "Witty Inventions."

After lunch, this humble man drove me to a Bradenton, Florida, Missionary Village. It was a subdivision of homes around a lake. Mr. Rossi donated the use of the homes to missionaries who had spent their lives on foreign soil while helping others. Usually, they did so with no care for their future retirement or consideration for how they would live when they could no longer serve others or endure the hardships of their mission work. Out of his abundance, he provided for them. They had a home to live in, and he had food delivered to their home daily to make sure they received at least one hot meal every day. Mr. Rossi also made annual trips back to his original home in Sicily, where he helped build a church and a mission. He was committed to using his resources to help others.

146

Coming from Sicily to New York and speaking no English, he told me he went to the public library to get information on this "Jesus" he heard so many talk about. He asked the librarian for a book about Jesus. He told me that one day, while reading between the book stacks, Jesus appeared to him and spoke to him. Mr. Rossi said he accepted Jesus into his heart and life, and he was never the same. That is why he believed God was the absolute source of all his blessings, finances, and inventions. He said he could never patent those ideas, for he wanted them to be used by all mankind.

I will be forever grateful to God to have witnessed the impact of the results of Proverbs 8:12, and to witness what it meant when it referred to "Witty Inventions." I am also thankful for the real life example of someone who experienced being the recipient and good steward of those Witty Inventions, the impact they could have on his life, and subsequently, the lives of others. My meeting with Mr. Anthony Rossi was one of the truly uplifting, extraordinary moments of my life. I never would have crossed paths with Mr. Rossi unless he sought me out because of a two-quarter gift to missionaries from my daughter. Now, you must admit that is extraordinary.

# HEALED of ALLERGIES

*"Is any sick among you? Let him call for the elders of the church;*
*and let them pray over him, anointing him with oil in the name*
*of the Lord; and the prayer of faith shall save the sick."* James 5:14-15

My youngest daughter, Christy, was always sneezing, coughing, and rubbing her eyes and nose. Growing up, she seemed to be allergic to everything. Every change of season in Atlanta, especially spring, brought pollen, pine dust, or something that made it difficult for her to sleep or sometimes even breathe.

When she reached age 4, my wife took her to be tested. They laid her on her stomach and scratched her back with over 50 different ingredients to see which one would trigger an infection and signal an allergic reaction for that pollen. All but one, 49 out of 50, flared up in an allergic skin reaction. It was worse than we thought. The doctor gave us medicine that had to be injected. Her mom and I practiced sticking needles into oranges so we could "punch" and give her the shots quickly, easily, and (our goal) pain free.

When it was time for a shot, I would clap my hands and say, "come to Daddy," and Christy would come running and jump into my arms. I would kiss and hug her closely, immobilizing her arm so her mom, Bertie, could come up behind her and jab her with the needle, quickly giving her the needed shot. She would scream and cry. After a number of these shots, Christy "wised up" and would not come to me when I called her. She would just shake her head "no" and I would go to her and pick her up. The ensuing shot in her arm from her mother would shock her back into "reality" of why I wanted to hold her. It got so bad, that even if there were no shots planned or due, Christy would not come to me, even if I simply wanted to hug her and love on her. We even tried her mom, Bertie, holding her for me to give her a shot to "trick" her. However, she got wise and would not even let her mom hold her if I was around her. She got wise to all our "tricks" to help her with those unwanted shots.

Then, it reached the point where Christy would actually run from me whenever she saw me. WOW ... just what a loving Dad lives for ... his daughter running from him every time she merely laid eyes on him. Spotting my presence would strike fear and cause her to flee from me. This was awful. We began to pray for a solution to this dilemma. This was no way to have a daughter respond to her parents' presence.

One Sunday, our pastor spoke on James 5:14-15, about calling the elders of the church to lay hands on the sick and pray for them; not placing faith in the faith of the elders, but in simple obedience to the biblical process.

James 5:14-15 says, *"Is any sick among you? Let him call for the elders of the Church; and let them pray over him, anointing him with oil in the name of The Lord; and, the prayer of faith shall save the sick ..."*

At that part of the sermon, my wife and I looked at each other, and we read each other's minds. "If we went to the elders, could Christy be healed?" Christy had been having regular allergy "scratch" tests, which showed that the shots were only preventing a couple of allergies, and lowering the strength of the reaction to others. However, nothing was making a strong difference. Over 45 of the 50 allergies tested for were not being eradicated or dealt with by the shots, and she had another round of scratch tests scheduled for Monday, the next day.

After church, we told the pastor our situation. We asked if he and the church elders would pray for Christy. He was delighted to have such an immediate response to his sermon. Someone *had* been listening. The pastor summoned the elders, who were scattered about the church talking to the attendees, to come up front. We picked up Christy. She knew we would never give her a shot in public ... in church. The elders and the pastor formed a close circle around us. The pastor took some olive "anointing" oil from a small bottle at the pulpit, touched Christy's forehead with it. While the elders laid hands on her, they all prayed for her healing. Just as quietly as it started, it was over. We did not "feel" anything. We did feel that we had acted in simple faith by simply being obedient to those verses the pastor spoke about in the book of in James.

On the way home, we discussed the prayer for healing we had experienced. We admitted that we did not "feel" anything. In fact, we confessed that if healing happened, it would not be because of our "faith", for we had none. We had struggled too long to even have hope that we could pick up and hold our daughter again, much less faith that she could be healed of all her allergies. What we did have was obedience to scripture, and a desire for Christy to be free of her allergies. I wanted to be able to approach and hold her without her fearing me, while her mother sneaked up behind her to give her a shot. At best, we could only agree we had faith that we were being obedient to God's Word heard in a sermon that day.

At the next day's visit to the doctor, Christy had no allergic reaction on her back to any of the 50 scratches. In fact, the doctor was so perplexed, he wanted to wait another week for the scratches in her back to heal up and then re-test her. He said, "Obviously, something went wrong with the test." My wife told the doctor about the prayers for healing from the elders that occurred the day before in Church. He said, "OK, miracles can happen. So, unless she has another reaction to anything, I don't need to see her again." We never took her back. Miraculously and instantly, Christy was healed of all her allergies.

When God heals, He does it completely and permanently. Today, Christy works with horses around hay and feed. She trains horses in all seasons and still has no allergies. I have seen students come into her barn with their heads swelled up from allergic reactions to the hay in the stalls. The possibilities for allergies are there, but non-existent in Christy. I learned that even if you do not have faith, extraordinary results can sometimes occur by simply following God's instructions, being obedient to His Word, and allowing His promises to work.

# FLIP A COIN FOR TAXES OWED

*"Render unto Caesar the things that are Caesar's."* Matthew 22:21

Are you kidding me? An IRS agent is having me flip a coin to determine my taxes owed.

The IRS challenged my tax returns going back five years. Because of the laws, my CPA, Kevin, had taken what he believed to be legitimate tax deductions, and I had no errors on my returns. Therefore, I challenged the IRS's position to allow me to take none of certain deductions over the five years they were reviewing. Their claim of additional taxes owed by me was because their viewpoint of the law differed from the viewpoint of my CPA, Kevin. The additional taxes the IRS said I owed for those back years ranged from an additional $3,200 lowest year, to over $14,000 highest year of the five years in question. Based upon my CPA's assurance of our position on the tax deductions being sound, he advised me to challenge it. We went to an IRS Office in Atlanta to meet with a Senior Agent to discuss our intended challenge in Tax Court for those five-year's taxes in dispute.

The interesting thing about going against any government agency in court is that you bear the brunt of 100% of all the costs ... on both sides! In this case, the IRS would use my tax dollars to fund their defense, while I am also obligated to pay 100% of my own legal fees, my CPA's fees and costs, and Court costs. In other words, if I question anything in court, I am obligated to pay 100% of everything to get fairness in my situation. Backed by everyone's taxes, the government ironically has the deepest pockets to defend their case, and even their appeal if they lose. It is a "no win" situation for the U.S. citizen.

That is not all! In addition, the agent notified us during our meeting that I would have to pay them the total of all the taxes for all five years in dispute, *up front,* before I could even file for my hearing in Tax Court. If I prevailed (won), I could then file all the paperwork again, and I could apply for a full refund for the portion I successfully defended. WOW … what a system! I pay for: my legal costs; my CPA's time; court costs; costs of the IRS's defense; and, I have to pay 100% of the taxes for five years I do not believe I owe in advance before I can even get into court to prove I don't owe them! Is this a fair and equitable system?

When we heard this, my CPA asked if he and I could step out into the hallway for a brief discussion. I told my CPA that although we both believed we were correct, and did not owe the taxes, I could in no way fund this fight financially under the terms the IRS imposed. After some time, we returned to the agent's office and argued profusely the unfairness of the terms and financial burden required to defend our position, especially since we felt we could win on all five-tax years in question. The IRS agent then admitted that in his personal opinion, we would have a good case if we could afford to get into tax court. Hearing that, but yet still knowing that I simply did not have the financial resources to challenge in court, my CPA and I pushed him to make some kind of a decision to settle this … now.

The agent's next move was unbelievable. He pulled a silver coin out of his desk and tossed it over to me. He said, "We'll flip a coin … you can call it heads or tails. Whoever wins the toss gets first choice of the five years to allow or drop, and then we'll alternate years from there." I looked at the astonished look on my CPA's face. When he got his composure, he nodded "yes" as if to say I *should* do this. Since I saw no way out of my financial dilemma, and under the pressure of the situation, as I flipped the coin I called "Heads." Heads it was, so I got first choice. Logically, I chose to throw out the payment owed on the highest year ($14,000). The IRS agent then picked the second highest year for me to have to pay. I then chose not to pay the third highest year, and so on. I got the first, third and fifth highest years to throw out for payment. The IRS got the second highest and fourth highest years owed for me to pay. He totaled the two years he selected and said, "That is what you owe." We settled.

The total amount owed for the two years he selected was less than one third of the total of all five years, had the IRS been correct. Even though I felt I owed nothing, I guess that is not such a bad deal, especially when I could not come up with all the up-front costs to challenge the IRS's position. However, back to the subject: Flipping a coin to determine my taxes owed ... *Really?* In the United States ... *Seriously?* What a country. Nevertheless, as Matthew 22:21 says, *"... render unto Caesar the things that are Caesar's ..."* Of my life's experiences, this goes down as one of the most extraordinary. I have never heard of anything quite like this before or since.

# DOUBLING

*"Give, and it shall be given unto you; good measure, pressed down, and shaken together, and running over, shall men give into your bosom. For with the same measure that ye mete withal it shall be measured to you again."* Luke 6:38

I had been in a total faith-walk in terms of giving. I began by trusting God to provide for me to give $1,000 away to my church. Before year-end, I was able to do that. Therefore, I thought it would be a big challenge to double that to $2,000. I made a faith pledge of that amount to the church our family was attending for their annual missions pledge drive, not knowing how in the world I could get $2,000 extra available cash in just one year. That was almost a third of my base salary of $600 per month. As an Account Executive (stockbroker) with Merrill Lynch, I was making a base of $600 per month, and I was eligible for a possible bonus (if earned). My wife and I had prayed all year for the extra $2,000 to come in, but now it was mid-December. There was no way we were going to be able to make the mission pledge by the end of the year. In fact, with my pay so low and with no bonus, it was impossible. The stock market was diving, the Dow Jones Industrial Average had dropped below 1,000, and business was so bad that no one in our Merrill Lynch office was making a bonus.

My manager called me in his office in December and told me to shut the door. He proceeded to tell me that although I had not earned a financial bonus, he was going to give me a bonus because I had been such a "positive, encouragement to the other men" in the boardroom during this market collapse. He told me not to tell anyone else what he was doing because it would be bad for morale. He then said the bonus amount was $2,000. WOW ... Just the amount of my pledge in my prayers. I left the manager's office floating on air. I went straight from his office into the marble men's restroom in the hall and wept. God had really answered our prayers. I could not wait to get to church on Sunday to make good on my mission pledge of $2,000. What a miracle.

I was on a roll! I proceeded to write a "contract" with God to more than double that faith pledge and told Him that if He would bless me with another $5,000 above my budget and tithes next year, I would give that away to missions also. Miraculously, by year-end, I had the $5,000 and gave it away. Now, I was really on a roll. I doubled my commitment to God to $10,000 the next year, and I told God I would give that amount away to some ministry if He provided it. However, I quit my job as stockbroker, and went into real estate syndication. I found out that when others ask you what you do and you respond with "I am Self-Employed," what is *really* happening is they view you as being "Unemployed."

In the interim, a national, Christian TV ministry invited my wife and me to a conference in Virginia with accommodations at the OMNI Hotel. At this time, we were unable to afford anything, even an evening dinner, so this was a nice treat. If we could afford the gas to drive there, all our expenses would be provided, including the hotel and meals. Therefore, we went. We considered it a "vacation" since we had been unable to afford doing anything like that.

They ministered to us for two days. On Saturday evening's final banquet, the head of the organization asked us to bow our heads and pray. Then, they told us to pick up our plate. Under it was a pledge card to make a faith pledge to their ministry over the next year. The shocking thing was that the minister said we could not trust God for a faith pledge of less than $10,000! They prayed, and everyone was to write down the amount of their faith pledge and fill in their information on the card. Then everyone was to take the card along with the candle at his or her place setting to the front of the ballroom, drop their pledge in a bowl, and light their candle from the Minister's larger candle. Everyone was to take the next place in a circle around the ballroom, everyone holding his or her lit candle while the music played.

I was sweating bullets since I realized this was getting way over my financial head. I lifted my bowed head and sneaked a peak. All the couples were lined up around the ballroom with their candles lit. Aside from my wife and me, the only other people who remained seated were a young couple at our table. During dinner conversation, the couple told us how broke they were. They finally found a trusted friend who would take their children for the three days. We told them that we were broke also, and whatever extra money we could scramble up was used to buy gas just to get there. Like them, we accepted the invitation as an expense-paid "mini-vacation." I have never been so embarrassed in my life ... music playing ... everyone else lined up around the perimeter of the ballroom with lit candles glowing, and us ... just sitting there in total humiliation. The minister then took the microphone to "remind" us that we were "Trusting God" in a "Faith" Pledge to provide that amount, and if HE did not provide it, then we were not obligated to give it. This was truly to be a total FAITH Pledge. That comment seemed to free us up to move, as we were not responsible and God was. If HE provided it, our only job was to give it.

In prayer, I already believed God for an extra $10,000, so I determined that this was just where we should give the amount we believed for in faith. Therefore, we wrote our "$10,000" Faith Pledge out on the card and proceeded to the front. We dropped

159

the card in the bowl, lit our candles, took our place with the others around the perimeter of the great ballroom, and joined in the singing. The tense air in the ballroom seemed to lighten up when the last two "hold-out" couples capitulated, pledged, lit their candles, and joined everyone else around the perimeter of the ballroom.

Well, that additional $10,000 pledge came in a sudden earned real estate commission, and I gave that away to fulfill my pledge to that ministry. NOW, I was REALLY on a role! As you can probably guess by now, I doubled my giving pledge again to $20,000 for the following year. I was going to believe God to provide more than I made last year in addition to what I needed to live on. After praying, I wrote the name of a ministry in Texas, teaching on faith that had blessed my life, and was coming to Atlanta to do a whole week's service in the OMNI. In faith, I wrote a check for $20,000 made out to that ministry and put it in my desk as part of that pledge. I pulled the check out of the drawer every morning, laid hands on it and prayed over it that God would provide the money to make that check good. I intended to give it to the Texas ministry toward the expenses of that week's crusade. Again, God came through with a real estate closing by the time the meetings came to Atlanta, and I was able give the $20,000 to them. Now I was becoming dangerous. I felt I could believe God for anything.

My trusting God for doubling the finances to give away ever-increasing amounts every year eventually resulted in high six-figured giving. Finally, a one million dollar gift of assets became the goal! I was learning to trust God to provide supernaturally to get the money to give ... to get again ... in order to give again. It is truly a sowing and reaping, ebb and flow of resources ... a flow that God wants us to get into. "We are "IN" the world," He says, "but not

"OF" the world." I believe He wants us to trust HIM, and trust IN Him. Moreover, He wants someone He can trust to funnel resources through to others. God is not a counterfeiter. He will not rain money from heaven. We must trust Him to speak to His people to be givers ... to be His conduits to get the finances to those who believe for them in their ministry.

I like the wording of II Corinthians 9:6-7 in the Amplified Bible (AMP), which says, *"Now, remember this: he who sows sparingly will also reap sparingly, and he who sows generously that blessing may come to others, will also reap generously and be blessed. Let each one give thoughtfully and with purpose, just as he has decided in his heart, not grudgingly or under compulsion, for God loves a cheerful giver and delights in the one whose heart is in his gift."*

God is good. I had started on a path of doubling annual faith pledges to give away to ministry, and God had miraculously provided for those faith pledges, year after year. The pledges were met through miracles and circumstances beyond my control. Because the arena I operated in was financial (Wall Street investments), that was my most skeptical area of life. I knew no one ever "gave" you anything ... you had to earn it. It only made sense that God would use that arena to prove to me that He was faithful, and that He would answer the prayers of those who truly trust Him.

It is extraordinary that I would make an innocent faith pledge in a year of devastating market collapse. Also extraordinary is that I would double the pledge and the pledge would be met. Then, in innocent, child-like faith, I would continue to double faith pledges every year. This eventually culminated in a gift of assets equal to a million dollars in value that would be given to a ministry. To an ordinary Oklahoma boy, that is extraordinary.

# GEMS

*"Take ye from among you an offering unto the Lord; whosoever is of a willing heart."* Exodus 35:5

Dr. Stanley preached eloquently about the opportunity that had arisen for First Baptist Church in Atlanta. The two square blocks behind the church were to become available, but our option to purchase it was for only 60 days. We needed to raise millions of dollars in the next 60 days to make the all-cash purchase required. Capital Cadillac had decided to move out of the downtown area and our church was given first crack at the purchase, but it was on unbelievable terms ... 60 days ... all cash. Dr. Stanley was making an analogy between this opportunity and the building of the temple, when everyone brought what they had; gold, silver, jewels ... whatever they had to help fund the building of the temple. Therefore, for the next 60-days, there would be security guards around a certain back door of the church for everyone to bring their valuables to donate toward the purchase of the Capital Cadillac property adjacent to the church.

For the next several Sundays, the offering consisted of members bringing their tithes, titles to property, titles to boats and automobiles, lake houses, and more, up to the front alter. There were diamond rings, gold, gold rings, jewelry, Rolex watches; sterling silver serving pieces ... even wedding bands. Just about everything imaginable. I got under conviction to do what I could do.

At the time, I was purchasing colored gemstones, such as Amethyst, Aquamarines, Tourmaline, and Imperial Topaz, directly from a mine owner in South America. This man also had his own cutters who cut the stones for him. I was buying the finished, cut

163

stones cheaply in bulk at only 10-12% of the appraised value here in the U.S. I would have them appraised by a qualified gem lab appraiser of a major jewelry chain, and then purchase huge volumes of them for cents on the dollar of appraisal. I would then mark them up to 25% of appraised value and sell them to investors, doubling my money, yet giving them gems appraised at 4-times their cost of purchase from me.  The investors would wait the appropriate legal time, and then donate them to a charity for a tax deduction based upon the appraised value. The investor would get a tax write-off for the appraised value, which would be 4-times the purchase price. Depending upon their tax bracket, they would at least double their return on investment via their tax deductions on the Gem donations.

I gathered all my inventory of gemstones with appraisals in a briefcase and went downtown to First Baptist to donate the gem inventory to the church. The appraised value of what I owned unsold to investors was over a million dollars. I found out later that a wealthy church member temporarily loaned the church the value of all the illiquid assets donated to the church (titles for boats, real estate, jewelry, and my gems, for example) so they could close on the property for cash. This allowed the church to make an orderly sale and liquidation of donated assets over time. They would not be financially impaired by suddenly "dumping" a bunch of property on the market under the duress of time urgency.

It felt good. I had never given away a million dollars worth of anything before. My actual cost of acquisition was approximately $200,000. I had never given away *that* much either.

The church made its goal in 60-days, and the property adjacent to the church was purchased. It stretched from behind First Baptist

164

a couple of blocks to Interstate I-85. It felt good to be a part of something so big where everyone in the church was making a sacrifice. Everyone brought an offering out of a willing heart. For me, it was extraordinary that I could donate assets valued at over a million dollars.

PAT ROBERTSON, President
CHRISTIAN BROADCASTING NETWORK
Guest Appearance: "700 CLUB" TV Show
September 29, 1982

**PAT ROBERTSON**
*Founder: 700 Club*
*Christian Broadcasting Network*

Picture hanging in my office reminds me of the power of prayer.
Taken September 29, 1982, with Pat Robertson on the set of The 700 Club TV show.

# The 700 CLUB

*"But without faith it is impossible to please him: for he that cometh to God must believe that He is, and that He is a rewarder of them that diligently seek Him."* Hebrews 11:6

Being in the investment world, I quickly learned that no one ever *"gave"* you anything. You had to plan, work, and fight for every dollar you got. I also learned that when you believed and received something from God, it was a supernatural manifestation from Him, because no one here on earth would ever just *give* you something. I believed I had a story to tell publically about giving generously and sacrificially while expecting nothing in return. In addition, because of the principle of sowing and reaping, God would provide not only the seed for sowing, but the harvest to be able to sow again.

I had been doubling the amount I gave each year for years as a pure act of faith. It resulted in being able to make a gift of over $1,000,000 in assets. I believed I had a story to tell the world about trusting God in faith for something so big, that you would know it was God when He answered the prayers. He would be the only explanation. Although I did not know how to reach the world, I did feel that the best, quickest way to get the message out was to be on the 700 Club with Pat Robertson. However, I did not know anyone at CBN, the Christian Broadcasting Network, nor did I know anyone who knew anyone there. Therefore, I committed to pray for me to appear on the 700 Club somehow. I prayed every morning for God to open the door to get an appearance on the 700 Club as a guest.

Secretly, I felt stupid. How could I, a young businessman who knew no one at CBN or the 700 Club, ever expect to get on the show? I prayed. I prayed every morning ... every morning for six months. Boy! I was glad I had told no one what I was praying for because a year had gone by. Based upon a year's passage with no results, they certainly would have questioned my prayer life (as a productive force that obtained results).

Eighteen months went by. Every morning I felt more stupid than the last. I had not even told my wife I was praying to be on the 700 Club. Twenty months ... then 24 months went by ... two full years of praying in faith. Then, my secretary told me to "take this call" ... it was someone "from the 700 Club."

The woman on the line identified herself as the Program Director of the 700 Club, and she advised it was suggested that I be a guest on the show. She said she would send me a packet of pages of information to fill out on myself ... my story. It also included questions I would like for Pat Robertson to ask me while on the air together with my responses to those questions in order to facilitate telling my story. Of course, my wife and others were surprised beyond belief, especially when I told her how I had been praying for this for over two years. I sent those questions in, and they flew my wife, Bertie, and me to Virginia Beach to be on the 700 Club TV show with Pat Robertson.

It just so happened that I was on the 700 Club during the annual, "7 Days Ablaze," the week when they would ask for funds and pledges to carry them through the full year. Talking about giving and trusting God in faith for continued increasing amounts to give seemed to strike a nerve with the viewers. The phones were ringing off the hook, and the pledges were great. In fact, the employees asked me to speak to them at the noon chapel. They closed the offices over the half hour's lunch, and I had the opportunity to speak to the entire CBN staff members.

My wife and I were provided with a ride back to the airport. Just before leaving, I asked the Program Director if she could tell me who suggested that I be a guest on the show. I told her that this was of most importance to me, since I did not have any connections at CBN or the 700 Club. Nor, did I even know anyone there to ask for me. She said, "Sure, I'll get that for you." She went back through double doors to her office. I could see her looking through her desk files and then cabinet files. She found nothing. She came out of her office and talked to two women on either side of the long aisle back to her office. Both of them began to look through their files. Again, they found nothing. This process repeated several times to no avail. The Program Director finally walked back out into the hallway, and said, "This is the strangest thing. This has never happened before. We have NO record of how we got your name as a suggested guest on the 700 Club."

As we rode to the airport to return to Atlanta, I was in shock. All I knew was I had prayed for two years asking God for exactly what occurred, and no one even had a record on how that had happened. We all know someone had to suggest me to be a guest, and I was upset that the station had no record of it. Later, upon reflection, I decided it was probably good that I had no one to thank … no one but God, that is. In fact, I called back two years later, and they still had no record of who suggested me to be a guest on the 700 Club TV Program. It was truly an extraordinary miracle in my life.

That successful answer to prayers was a life-changer for me. At that point, I KNEW that with God, I was a majority. With God, nothing was going to be impossible, for with Him all things are possible to them that believe. In addition, "*Without Faith, it is impossible to please Him. For whosoever comes to God must believe that He IS (God) and that He IS a rewarder of those who diligently seek Him.*" Hebrews 11:6

Another remarkable thing about this story is that they planned to have me on the show during the week of faith pledges, but just had not asked me yet. Here I was being faithful in prayer every day to ask God to do something that He had already done. I just did not know about it. I think that God was allowing me to be faithful in prayer, even though unknowingly, the answer was already there.

I have a photo hanging in my office, taken in 1982, while standing with Pat Robertson on the 700 Club set. It is there as a reminder to me that God can answer prayers of faith, regardless of how absurd they are or how impossible they seem to be. That was an extraordinary answer to prayer for me.

# PERCEPTION is REALITY

We were careful to refrain from emphasizing money or material things (possessions) to our daughters. Our success at this became evident one night at the dinner table when our youngest daughter, Christy, began telling the story of her friend in high school. The friend told Christy how embarrassed she was for her prom date to pick her up at her home, because it was so large and beautiful. It seems she did not want her date to be intimidated or think she was rich, but just wanted to be treated like a normal person by her date. Christy then said, "Can you imagine how hard it will be for her and how uncomfortable she will be? There is just no way she could live this down. She is even thinking about giving her prom date the address of a friend and having him pick her up for prom at that place."

We asked Christy if she knew what her friend's house looked like. She said, "Oh yes." She then described how her friend's house was over 5,000 square feet on a whole acre lot, with a circular drive in front of it. Christy told us how sorry she felt for her friend, and how she was glad she wouldn't have to ever be put in that dating situation herself.

My wife and I just looked at each other, not knowing what to say. We knew we were both thinking, "Yes, we did it… she is clueless about her own situation." I was thinking, "Our home was 11,000 square feet on 32 acres, a quarter of a mile drive through iron gates to a circular drive that had 12 parking spaces." We had silk fabric made into wallpaper from the matching silk backing on the French dining room chairs. We had five fireplaces, a 3,000 square foot office wing with a conference room, and 22 ½ tons of air conditioning with five zone controls. There was a basement with a billiard room, 10 ft. high ceilings, and a full kitchen with bar seating for ten. Finally, we had a 2,500 square foot guest cabin, a barn with eight stalls, and a full riding ring for equestrian training. I was thinking about what a good job we had done to downplay and act casual about our accommodations, so much that Christy would not even make the connection between where she lived, and the empathy and concern for her friend being embarrassed to be picked up for a date at her home, because of the opulence.

Finally, I broke my thought to say, "Christy, you could have the same problem as your friend. Look at what you're living in." Christy, who was totally into the care, feeding and riding of her horses said, "Dad, it's not the same thing. We live on a farm."

"Yes," I thought, "We have done a fantastic job at down-playing our surroundings to our kids, so much so that they didn't even realize they were living in a larger home than their friends."

We had succeeded in not discussing or drawing attention to material things and emphasized that people were the most important thing. At that moment, I was not only proud of my daughters, but I had a deep sense of satisfaction. My wife and I had done a good job of parenting. With the environment we had created, my daughter's perception of being on a "farm" was reality for her … no thought of size.

# PAYING for PRAYING

*"Withhold not good from them to whom it is due,
when it is in the power of thy hand to do it."* Proverbs 3:27

In a cafeteria booth in Atlanta, I saw a young couple with very little to eat bow their heads and ask the blessing on the meager amount of food they had on their trays. I estimated that there could not be even $10 worth of food between them. I got up, went over to their booth and said, "I am an Atlanta businessman, and I noticed you bowed your heads in this public place to ask the blessing on your food. I applaud those who are not ashamed to pray in public, so I always try to buy the meals for those I witness doing that. Here is $10 to cover your meal, plus a $2 tip to leave for the waitress."

After the shock wore off, they began to cry. They shared with me that they were discussing ending their marriage because they just did not see any way to make it work. They expressed that nothing positive seemed to work in their lives. After this encounter, they agreed that they were going to try once again to make it work. They were warmed by this gesture. I do not know what became of them or their marriage, but it felt good to do that positive deed.

Another time, in a cafeteria while on a business trip in Indianapolis, Indiana, I saw a very elderly couple grasp hands, bow their heads and pray a blessing before they began to eat. I quickly assessed the value of their meals together, and walked over to them with a $20 bill and laid it on the table. "I am an Atlanta businessman," I said, "and I applaud those who are not ashamed to pray in public, so I always try to buy the meals for those praying when I witness it. Here is $20 to cover your meal plus tip."

173

They both looked up with tears in their eyes and told me they were being evicted from their home and needed a sign that God had not forgotten about them. They were out of food and only had $20 to get something to eat. They decided to "splurge" and eat out at the cafeteria because they did not have enough money to go to a regular restaurant. They both expressed gratitude for the money, but mostly for the "sign" that God had not forgotten about them. They were encouraged by my random act of kindness.

It is always gratifying to me when I am at a public restaurant and see folks at a table, whether a couple, family, or a large group, bow their heads to ask God's blessing on their meal. I always wished I could reinforce this bold action on behalf of the Christian world. Do not be ashamed in public to say "grace" before a meal, as you probably do at home. I began making it a practice to buy the meals for those I see pray before their meals in a public restaurant.

My commitment was tested one night in a Steak & Ale Restaurant in Atlanta. I was in a booth and had just ordered, when a large group of 10 people was seated in the back room near me. It appeared to be either family or a large business group from an office. As I was nearing the end of my meal, the party of ten was served. When the waiters set the last plate down, the man at the head of the table had everyone grasp hands on either side of them and the whole circle bowed their heads while he prayed. I thought, "Oh no. This is going to cost me." I went over to the alcove where their server was and told her what I wanted to do. I asked if she could estimate the approximate value of their meal. She did, and I put $250 on my credit card, plus a 20% tip of $50. The server was flabbergasted. She said she had never heard of anyone doing this before. This was a first for her. I then went over to the table with the receipt, handed it to the head of the table and told them what I

174

had done and why ... my response to seeing them praying publically for their meal. Everyone was grateful, especially the man at the head of the table.

Paying for their meal brought me so much pleasure and satisfaction. Now, I am running a non-profit and not making the money I used to do in business, so I do not have the financial latitude to do that anymore. However, if I ever have the surplus means to reinstitute that practice, I will do so. It was fun and was one of the most rewarding things I have done in my lifetime. You should try it! It makes an extraordinary impact on those you recognize in this way.

*(Left to Right)* Georgia Congressman, John Linder, Dean O. Webb, Rev. Pat Robertson ... Taken during the 1988 New Orleans National Convention

# 1988 NEW ORLEANS NATIONAL CONVENTION

*"For the ways of men are before the eyes of the Lord,
and he pondereth all his goings."* Proverbs 5:21

How can I describe the electricity of thousands of delegates from all 50 states and territories crowded into the New Orleans Super Dome? Everyone was using noisemakers and blowing horns. Bands were playing, nationally known TV anchors walked up and down the aisles followed by men with huge TV cameras on their shoulders pointed toward the anchors while interviewing delegates live, on national TV. To be on the convention floor experiencing, firsthand, what it was like to be an elected delegate to a National Political Convention was an exciting and memorable experience. Actually, to be one of 3,000 or so people representing about 100 million people in electing a Party's Presidential candidate is an extraordinary opportunity.

In 1988, Georgia had an allotment for a total of 40 delegates for the whole state. My wife, Bertie, and I had campaigned and lobbied to be successfully elected from our district as two of the 40. Each delegate was allowed to bring a guest, so my wife and I each took one of our daughters, and our whole family was at the convention together. Although George Bush was the leading Republican candidate, we were both pledged to presidential candidate, Pat Robertson. The main-line Republican Party delegates for Bush looked upon all of the Robertson delegates with disdain. In fact, the Robertson supporters had turned out in such huge numbers, that we controlled the Georgia State Convention, which angered the old, long-time party members. They responded by holding a second "rump" convention, and locked out all known Robertson supporters from that "convention." We took our convention's actions to court and won as being the legitimate convention over the "rump" convention. The Party had to allow us to attend the National Convention as official delegates, which they did not like. The party regulars treated us, the Robertson delegates, like second-class citizens.

In spite of the inner-party struggles between the old-time Republicans and the new "Christian right" supporters of Pat Robertson, we had fun. We were wined and dined by all of the candidates and those with political ambitions desiring to be noticed for their future campaign runs. At one party, I remember vividly, we were bused to a mansion on ten acres. When we pulled up, the U.S. Catamaran scheduled to represent the United States of America in the America's Cup was in front of the home to the right of the sidewalk leading to the house. Our entry "ticket" was for each delegate to sign our names on the sail for good luck in the race. We then went through the home and out the back door. There were white tents placed all around the huge backyard. Because of the extreme humidity in New Orleans, all of the tents had flooring, clear plastic sides that dropped down, and air conditioning piped and blowing into each tent. Each tent had a different band playing different styles of music for the type of cuisine in each tent. There was New Orleans Jazz for the tent with Creole; Blues music in the tent with Bar-B-Q; a big band sound for the American cuisine, and so on. It was a sumptuous feast and memorable festivity. No wonder the party regulars did not want to give up their delegate seats to these new, passionate Christians supporting Pat Roberson. Every day was full of invitations to sumptuous feasts and spectacular parties between speeches in a filled Super Dome where few of the delegates on the convention floor totally listened.

The Party scheduled the speaking slots, and placed Pat Robertson in an afternoon slot that had no national TV network coverage at that time. Pat negotiated a trade of his hundreds of pledged delegates over to George Bush in exchange for a prime-time slot for his speech. This got his message heard during prime time. It avoided a floor fight, which put forth the appearance of solidarity for Bush. Pat did not have enough delegates to be effectual anyway, so it was a win-win for everyone.

A prime benefit of being an elected delegate to your party's national convention is ... if your party candidate wins the national election for President, you automatically receive an invitation for each delegate and a guest to attend the President's Inaugural Ball, together with the entire week's inaugural activities in Washington, D.C. in January, including swearing the President into office. George Bush did win. Bertie and I received invitations to all the inaugural week festivities with our two-guest allowance; meaning our two daughters experienced the whole week of events with us. It was one of the most memorable weeks of our lives; an extraordinary experience that few get to experience in a lifetime.

Pictured above in front of the Whitehouse
Below was received from President Bush for supporting him.

TO: Mr. Dean Webb

Thank you for your support. Together we can build a single nation of justice and opportunity.

Warmest regards,

Photo Number: 1116717-258013070

# NIGHT BEFORE THE PRESIDENT'S INAUGURAL WALK

*"Wise men lay up knowledge...." Proverbs 10:14*

We were almost too excited to sleep. My wife and I were in the Washington D.C. hotel with our two daughters trying to get some sleep before the big day tomorrow ... the swearing in of George H.W. Bush as the 41$^{st}$ President with Dan Quayle as his Vice President. They would then take the long walk to the White House down Pennsylvania Avenue, lined by thousands of celebratory well-wishers. Following that, we had invitations to attend the President's Inaugural Ball.

My wife and I campaigned to be two of the 40 Delegates elected at the State of Georgia Republican Convention to represent Georgia to the Republican National Convention, which was in New Orleans at the Super Dome. Since the Republican candidate won the national presidential election in November 1988, Delegates were given invitations to attend the weeklong Inaugural festivities in Washington, D.C. in January 1989. Each Delegate could bring one guest each, so they could attend with their spouse. However, since Bertie and I were both Delegates, we each brought one of our two daughters as our guests to the nation's capital to experience the rare treat of being an invited guest to all inaugural events, all week long. The only thing we had to "elbow" our way to with general admission tickets was the incredible fireworks display above the Washington Mall. For everything else, we had reserved seats.

My youngest daughter, Christy, *was* too excited to sleep. At 3:00 am, I woke up to her whisper, "Dad, Dad, wake up." When I did, she asked me if I would go downstairs with her to the street to look around. She just wanted to experience the quiet of our nation's Capital and Pennsylvania Avenue before the crowds began lining the street to catch a glimpse of the newly elected President of the United States. We dressed warmly. When the elevator deposited us on street level and we walked out onto the sidewalk and over to Pennsylvania Avenue, I was shocked. I have never seen such a beehive of "official" activity going on at that hour of the night in my life. Washington, D.C. police, military units, swat teams in black were checking every possible hiding place along the parade route. Huge tanker trucks full of hot wax were rolling slowly down the parade route. As trashcans were emptied, a man guided a hose from the tanker truck to pump a seal of hot wax around the lids and openings. The cans remained visible in their normal placement, but were not usable. No one could use them to hide or place a bomb explosive to harm the people or the President along the Inaugural Parade route. On TV, everything would look normal.

Manhole covers were pried open in the street, and military and swat teams were going down the stair ladders into the caverns below the street with huge lights, checking for people and objects … anything out of place or suspicious. Upon returning up to street level and giving the "all clear," the hot wax was pumped through a hose to seal the manhole covers in place, making it safe for the new Presidential party to walk or drive over.

I then saw a red dot moving on my daughter's coat. I turned around as my eyes followed the infrared sighting back to the origin. A sniper was on the roof of a building across the street. That is when I noticed many infrared dots floating around the street. The snipers, tasked with protection of the new President, were all along the parade route on both sides of the street, adjusting their scopes and sightings in protection response preparation for tomorrow's Presidential parade.

Those dark hours of early morning exposed a world we did not know existed. We were not aware of the extreme measures taken behind the scenes to protect our President. Experiencing this activity first hand and up close was extraordinary. It was an experience that I would have slept through and never seen or known existed if Christy had not been too excited to sleep. I am glad I did not sleep through it.

It was an awesome, extraordinary, informative, and clearly memorable experience. Proverbs 10:14 says, *"Wise men lay up knowledge."*

At the Inaugural Ball with my wife, Bertie and my daughters,
Christine and Catherine.

# THE INAUGURAL BALL

*"She seeketh wool, and flax, and worketh willingly*
*with her hands."* Proverbs *31:13*

Hard to believe, but here we were in Washington, D.C., dancing at the Inaugural Ball of newly elected President George H.W. Bush. Hard to believe, because we were broke. However, here we were; my wife and two daughters, swirling in gorgeous ball gowns; gowns that were stunning and equal to any other gown in beauty in that huge Inaugural Ballroom. If we were broke, how could we be here in this limited, invitation only access venue, in relative luxury?

When our invitations to attend the President's Inaugural Ball arrived, there was no way to afford a ball gown to attend, much less three of them. Realizing that this might be a once in a lifetime opportunity that would never present itself to us again, (and, it never did) my wife sprung into action writing down ideas, sketching out designs, looking at magazines, and taking measurements of herself and my daughters.

In a visit to her sister, Camilla, in Miami, my wife went to fabric shops owned by Cubans. There, they had magnificent sheers she purchased to use for sleeves and other equally unusual fabric for the gown bodies. She created and sewed three beautiful ball gowns that compared favorably to all the other gowns at the Inaugural Ball. To get ideas, she had gone to look at gowns before designing theirs. She knew she was looking at gowns out on the dance floor that were thousands of dollars each. The three of them in their gorgeous ball gowns fit in nicely. She had done what was necessary to seize the moment of opportunity that we knew was an invitation of a lifetime.

185

Sometimes you can build an exciting memory by not being intimidated by your financial circumstances and just doing whatever you can do resourcefully to take advantage of the extraordinary opportunity. That one opportunity, which may not knock on your door again, will provide you with a lifetime of unforgettable memories. For us, we will never forget the Inaugural Ball. Yet, if we had not pushed, and been resourceful to get there, we would not even have a frame of reference to know what an extraordinary experience we would have missed.

My wife, Bertie, was a living example of Proverbs 31:13 that says, *"She seeketh wool and flax, and worketh willingly with her hands."*

Pictured with Robert Gates, Secretary of Defense

Pictured with Zell Miller, Georgia Governor and U. S. Senator

187

Pictured with Sarah Palin, Alaska Governor
and Vice Presidential candidate in 2008.

Pictured with Newt Gingrich, former Speaker of the House

189

Pictured with Jack Kemp, pro football player, Congressman,
Cabinet Secretary and Vice-Presidential candidate

190

# POWER

I have heard it said that when businessmen have accomplished all they can in the business world, the next level of power is politics. I once read about a "State" Representative in California, who spent $17 million dollars to run for a California State legislative position that paid only $18,000 a year. No one is that crazy unless they simply seek power. Remember, this was not a U.S. Representative position ... it was only a State position.

I experienced the powerful in a most unusual way. My wife, Bertie, and I were invited to the Presidential Inauguration week of Inauguration activities in January 1989. We were in Washington, D.C. for the Inaugural week and had to grab lunch one day before the next scheduled event. We started to the restaurant early so we would have no trouble getting a table. We decided to try the Old Ebbitt Grill near the White House, established in 1856. It was full of history since Presidents Grant, Cleveland, Harding and Theodore Roosevelt had eaten there. It is still a popular meeting site for political insiders and other power brokers. We wanted to try it since we might never have the opportunity to be in Washington, D.C. together again.

When we got inside the Old Ebbitt Grill at 11:00 am, they said, "Sorry, but we are full." I looked around and they were empty. There was not a single seat or table occupied in the entire restaurant. We arrived so early that we had beaten everyone there. In fact, they were just completing their table set-ups. "What do you mean you're full? There is no one here," I said. Again, the hostess said, "I'm sorry but we are full." I said, "We came early enough to beat the entire crowd, and it looks like we did." She still said she could not seat us. I pushed her to seat us back by the kitchen door, and told her that we would order whatever the waitress said could be fixed the quickest, so we would not be here long. "In fact," I said, "We have to be going to an event that starts at noon, so we cannot be here long." She finally said, "OK," and sat us in the back behind a barrier wall which shielded the view of the kitchen door, but the wall also blocked the rest of the restaurant from our view.

On the way to our table, we passed row after row of empty tables. I wondered, "Who could be powerful enough to make reservations that would cause an empty restaurant to turn away business at 11:00 am?"

We enjoyed our sandwiches and got up to leave and pay the bill. As we rounded the corner of the wall we were seated behind, I got cold chills. The restaurant was now packed. There was not one empty seat anywhere. However, as I looked around closely, here was my answer. Seated were Senators, members of the House, one and two star generals, and all-powerful people in Washington. Now I knew "Power."

When we stepped outside, it was also amazing. Dozens of limos and town cars lined up in double rows blocking the two closest lanes, with men in dark suits standing or leaning against the front fenders, while waiting for those inside to finish their "power lunch" and business. After lunch, they would be whisked away to the next engagement of the important people's business. They kept a famous restaurant empty and turning away business ... now, that is power! Those are our representatives, paid by us to be there, wielding their power. It seemed distorted. It made me sick.

It made me upset. Washington, D.C. is certainly dysfunctional, at least compared to the way the rest of the country lives ... the ones who elect them to office so they can be there. It is no wonder some of us feel that those who go to Washington, D.C. to represent us seem to appear extraordinarily disconnected from reality and the "real" world. Maybe they are!

# ROLEX PROSPECTING

*"Seest thou a man diligent in his business?*
*He shall stand before kings."* Proverbs 22:29

Who did he think he was? Here was an arrogant, full-of-himself Texan, only age 23, insisting that he be allowed to become a Stockbroker with Merrill Lynch, then the largest securities firm in the world. When I went to work as a stockbroker for Merrill Lynch in 1968, they required that one be at least age 25 to enter training. They reasoned that if you were going to be managing millions of dollars for businessmen and others, you must at least "appear" to have some experience in life. Here was this guy, Tom from Texas, insisting that Merrill Lynch make an exception for him and give him a waiver to begin working at age 23. He would not take "no" for an answer.

Without going into detail, after some months, Merrill Lynch relented and gave Tom the waiver he was lobbying for, and he went to work. Of course, as a conditional employee, he was on probation for the first six months depending upon results and performance. He astonished everyone in the boardroom, because he quickly passed both the new and the long-time brokers in the office, with millions of dollars under his management. He was out of the office a lot, more than the rest of us. We all had to be out prospecting and meeting new people in order to gain business for ourselves, but this was ridiculous. Tom was gone almost half of each day, but he was bringing in hundreds of thousands of dollars under his management. While we spent hours analyzing the market for profitable trades to endear our clients to us, Tom was conservative. He put his clients into bonds for interest, not to risk losing any money, but certainly not trading to make money for his clients like the rest of us. It was a very competitive business. It was not unusual to have your account stolen away and transferred to another brokerage firm by a stockbroker who promised to make a client more money than you were making him.

After two years, I asked Tom how he was able to bring in so much money under his management in new accounts, especially since he was so young ... and looked it. However, he refused to tell me his "secret" of prospecting. He was obviously doing something very well, convincing, or creative in order to get the huge amount of dollars under management so quickly compared to others who had been in the business for dozens of years. He was setting the world on fire, and the other 35 brokers in our trading boardroom knew he was out-classing us all in the prospecting hunt for money to manage.

One day, after many requests of Tom, he finally agreed to let me in on his little secret of prospecting for new accounts provided I would not tell anyone else, nor use his method for myself. I agreed, and because of my intense curiosity, he finally told me his secret. In addition, I have never, before or since, heard of a more effective sales prospecting tool than Tom's little secret.

Are you ready? Here it is. Tom pulled out a diamond Presidential Rolex watch valued at over $25,000. (Today's value is $48,000 plus.) He said, "Instead of buying a house when I moved to Atlanta, I bought this $25,000 Diamond Rolex. When I prospect, I go to the head of the company's secretary outside his office and hand her this Rolex. I then say, 'I need to see Mr. _____, (her boss's name), and I want you to hand him this Presidential Rolex. Tell him that I only want 5-minutes of his time, and if I take a second longer, the watch is his to keep.' After the secretary's eyes

196

narrow back to normal from bugging out at the diamonds on the bezel along with the diamond pave' surface of the watch with the diamond band, she takes the risk of going into the CEO's office and interrupting him with the message and handing him the watch." Tom said, "Almost 100% of the time, the executive will tell his secretary to have me come on in."

Tom said he has a stopwatch in his left hand at his side, which he punches when he crosses the threshold of the office and extends his right hand to shake the executive's hand in greeting. He then gives him his speech about how he is a large bond trader and can make him lots of money on initial offerings of bonds offered net at par with no commission, gain interest on the bonds, and all without taking any risks with the man's principle. After about four minutes or so, Tom would raise his left hand and click the stopwatch to show the executive that he kept his promise to be under the five-minute limit. Then he would request his Rolex back. While the executive sadly gives up the diamond watch, which he surely thinks he would be able to keep, Tom exchanges his watch for his business card, and simply says, "Call me if you really want to make money." Tom thanks the executive and leaves. The executive probably has never heard any salesman keep a proposal to less than five minutes. He probably thought it was a slam-dunk and that he was going to be able to keep the diamond Rolex.

Tom said it was rare when an executive he prospects does not call him back within a week for another meeting to open an account. In addition, if he does not, Tom calls him within 10 days to ask for his business. He said the executives always remember the "Rolex Guy" and is impressed with his brashness and creativity in comparison to the other brokers prospecting him. Tom said he usually gets the business account, and since it is not a risky

197

investment, he usually opens an account for a lot of money, far larger than the rest of us were able to do. You must admire the creativity and brashness of Texans.

In less than 4 years, Tom went on to another brokerage firm with almost a million dollar transfer bonus to jump ship on Merrill Lynch. He was that much of an asset to a Wall Street firm. Although he was not supposed to take his clients with him, most of them initiated the action to follow him to the new brokerage firm of employment. I will never forget him and his extraordinary, creative way to prospect for new business.

# ANNUAL FATHER'S DAY

*"And the glory of children are their fathers."* Proverbs 17:6

We got "married" every Father's day. My wife, daughters and I attended Dr. Charles Stanley's church in downtown Atlanta for 14 years. Although we lived out beyond Stone Mountain, Georgia, it was worth the nearly hour's drive downtown every Sunday to listen to Dr. Charles Stanley's message. Father's Day Sunday evening was particularly special because we renewed our wedding vows annually, every Sunday evening on Father's Day. The whole church really made it a big deal.

All married couples dressed up in their wedding attire (if it still fit) or in their most formal, best or Sunday attire. They decorated the church with flowers, a white wedding arch, candles, and everything you would expect to see in a large, 3,000-seat sanctuary for a wedding. While all children would sit upstairs in the large, horseshoe-shaped balcony around the sides and back of the auditorium, the couples would all file in to the wedding march and fill in the entire downstairs of the sanctuary.

They held an entire wedding ceremony, with love songs and beautiful music. Dr. Stanley would then have us all stand, face our mates, clasp hands, and repeat our wedding vows after him. After he pronounced us "re-joined together again due to our re-commitment," we would then do a processional to music out the front of the church into a fully decorated gymnasium-type auditorium, again fully decorated with multiple tiered wedding cakes, punch, and arches covered in white roses. There were photographers to capture each couple's picture under an arch. The children had followed us out of the auditorium and joined us in the

199

wedding reception. It was a happy moment we all looked forward to enjoying each year.

Dr. Charles Stanley focused his sermons, his churches' activities and events around the men and fathers in the church. I guess he figured that if the men were involved, the entire family unit would be involved and would benefit so much. When I look back, I do not know how I would have raised my two daughters to be the persons they are without sitting under the ministry of Dr. Stanley. In Proverbs 17:6, it says, *"the glory of children are their fathers."* It makes sense to concentrate on the fathers to leave their children a legacy to be proud of when memories manifest throughout their lives.

How blessed I was to sit under the weekly ministry of Dr. Charles Stanley. His instruction to fathers was so practical in raising children. It did not hurt that we re-did our wedding vows each year as a couple, recommitting to our vows as our children of that union watched from the balcony. Father's Day under the ministry of Dr. Charles Stanley was always special and quite an extraordinary event.

# OXEN IN THE STALL

*"Where no oxen are, the crib is clean: but much increase is by the strength of the ox."* Proverb 14:4

I went to First Baptist Church in downtown Atlanta to pick up my pastor, Dr. Charles Stanley, to go to lunch. As I pulled up in my car to pick him up, I realized my car was a mess. In the real estate business, you work on many projects at once. I had files stacked within easy reach on the front seat, the front floor, and the back seat. As he opened the front door to get in, he had to wait while I put the car in park, and he watched as I scrambled to pick up files and put them in the back seat. I was flustered and embarrassed to have his entry delayed by my having to move all the paperwork to clear the seat for him to sit. After all, it had taken months of lead-time to get an appointment with this busy pastor. I was driving a Mercedes, but it might have well been a garbage truck due to stacks of paper and files.

Dr. Stanley put me at ease quickly, overriding my multiple apologies by saying, "Don't worry about it. Much increase comes from an occupied crib." I knew he was referencing Proverbs 14:4, which says, *"Where no oxen are, the crib is clean; but much increase is by the strength of the ox."* That comment put me at ease instantly, and I appreciated the response.

Since then, it seems that I am always working on multiple projects at the same time, even to this day. Now, my excuse for my desk piled high with work is a quote from Dr. Albert Einstein when he said, "They say a cluttered desk is an indication of a cluttered mind. What does that say about an empty desk?" That works for me.

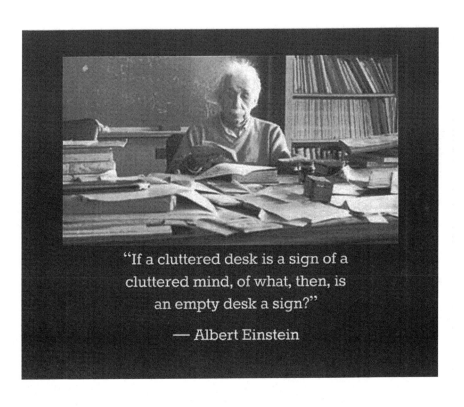

"If a cluttered desk is a sign of a cluttered mind, of what, then, is an empty desk a sign?"

— Albert Einstein

# FASTING "TRICK"

*"Is this not the fast that I have chosen?"* Isaiah 58:6

Our hearts sank, as we turned to look at each other in church. Our Pastor, Dr. Charles Stanley, had just requested that the whole church fast the following week and pray. Normally, we would have been eager to do anything he said. However, of *all* weeks, we were leaving for a week's vacation at the beach in Florida. Our beach vacations always included lots of eating fresh seafood and other delicacies because we dined out at a different place every night. Our custom, in fact, was to check into the condominium on the beach and then return to the mainland  grocery store. It was our tradition to let down our "eating guard" and let the girls pull every treat and goody from the shelves that they desired to munch on, and fill the basket with every treat that would be restricted from them the rest of the year. It was a free-for-all culinary rampage. Actually, my wife and I indulged also. It was our time to indulge and eat special treats ... all week long.

That bubble popped as we realized that we were asked to eat nothing ... Nothing ... for a *whole week*. We did not mind the fast. It was just the timing of the vacation week.  We did not want to be out of sync or out of unity with the rest of the church. Dutifully, we committed to fast and pray during meals our whole vacation week at the beach.  We did not put that obligation on our daughters. We just did it ourselves. Forgoing fresh seafood, and watching them eat all those chips and cookies was the most difficult thing we have ever done. Nevertheless, we did it. We made it through the whole vacation week without eating, just fasting.

When we returned home and went to church the following Sunday, we wondered if everyone else in the church had made the same commitment we had made. We felt our week of fasting certainly had to be more difficult since we did it during our vacation week at the beach.

When we got out of our Sunday school class, we entered the vestibule, the large area between the front door and the doors to the back of the Sanctuary. There, we spotted a huge board, broken down into days of the week, with 24-hour time slots below each day. In each hourly time slot was the name of a person or couple. The entire grid was filled with names. We asked an usher what that was since we had been on vacation the previous week. The usher said, "You know that Dr. Stanley wanted the whole church to fast for the week, and this is the sign-up commitment grid to ensure that at least one person would be fasting and praying every hour during the whole week."

WHAT? My wife and I fasted the entire week on vacation while the balance of the 3,000-plus member church split up the week into one-hour segments between them to fast and pray. WOW. How big of a misunderstanding can one have in a church pew? Maybe more details were explained later, and we missed it because we were gone. We were shocked that we could have missed the task that far off base. In retrospect, was it harmful that we fasted ... prayed more ... experienced the self-discipline? I think not. Secretly, we felt tricked. After the fact, the fasting was good for us to do. The two of us equaled the whole church's commitment by ourselves. Looking back, it seems just plain funny, but not at the time! At the time, we felt that we had accomplished an extraordinary feat.

# CINNAMON SUGAR III

*"He sent His Word, and healed them."* Psalms 107:20

We had a registered collie named Cinnamon Sugar the 3<sup>rd</sup>. She looked just like Lassie. We got her as a pup and raised her. She was our daughter's best friend. She was gentle, kind and loving. She was like another family member to us.

She began acting funny and took her to the veterinarian to be checked out. The vet told us she had heartworms and had to be "put down." We left the vet's office with our Cinnamon Sugar and refused the suggested demise. The vet was upset that we left with our diseased dog instead of "putting her down."

I looked up all the scriptures on healing and recorded them on cassette, reading them in sequence, repeatedly, until I had filled an hour cassette with healing scriptures read by me. We then locked the dog in the garage and turned on the tape. We played the tape for hours and hours, day and night. Cinnamon Sugar III could not get away from the Bible scriptures on healing. Every night, she was inundated with a continuous loop of recorded scriptures being read from the Bible on healing. My premise was if Psalms 107:20 were true, *"He sent His Word and healed them,"* then His Word could heal our dog.

Meanwhile, we kept receiving calls from our veterinarian saying that we must bring our dog in to be euthanized, or she would report us. She said that if our dog excreted in a neighbor's yard and their dog got near it, they could get heartworms also. She said we could be causing an epidemic within the neighborhood.

When we did not respond to that, she threatened to call all the neighbors and tell them what we were doing and how irresponsible we were being. She treated most of the pets in our neighborhood, and we knew that she had their phone numbers. She said our dog would die anyway. She asked why we did not just bring her in.

After a couple of months, we laid hands on Cinnamon Sugar III again. We prayed for her healing in addition to the days and nights of scriptures played over her. We finally took her back to the vet, but only with the condition of testing her again. Although she protested and said it would not do any good, she finally agreed that if we brought her back in, she would test her again for heartworms. Therefore, we did and she tested her. Again, against the vet's will, we would not leave the dog with her, but took her home while we waited for the lab results.

She finally called us and asked what we did to her. She said the results showed NO heartworms at all, even though she was sure of the initial diagnosis. She even double-checked it. We told her what we did with the round-the-clock healing scriptures played on cassette. She was in disbelief. She had never heard of anything like that before. We admitted that we had not either.

We kept our beloved collie, Cinnamon Sugar III, for many more years of enjoyment as our family pet. Moreover, we will never forget the answer to prayer and God's response to our simple faith placed in Him and His Word. I do not know if this is a "formula" for healing pets. I sure would not start another "pet healing" religious denomination based upon this experience. What I do know is that God honors simple faith placed in Him and His Word. Our simple, blind, unwavering faith in the healing power of the Word of God healed our collie. To our veterinarian, we seemed crazy. However, to us at the time, we felt normal... just simply trusting God and His Word. It was an extraordinary experience for the vet, Cinnamon Sugar III and us.

# YOUR SCALP IN YOUR FACE

*"For who knoweth what is good for man in this life?"* Ecclesiastes 6:12

I just cannot describe the terror I felt when I woke up in the middle of my operation and sat straight up on the operating table. The hair on the top of my head was pulled down over my face ... in my face. To get at the bone fragments in my crushed forehead, they had shaved my scalp in a strip over the top curve of my head in a straight line from ear to ear. Then they made an incision ear to ear across the top of my skull. Finally, they pulled the skin and scalp, hair and all, down over the front of my face to get to my forehead.

When scheduled for double surgery, hernia and cranial, the big concern was how much anesthesia to give me. I have Sleep Apnea, so I sleep on a CPAP (Constant Positive Air Pressure) machine. Too much anesthesia and I might not wake up because of the Apnea. Too little, and I would not be fully "out" and would feel intense pain from the two surgeries going on simultaneously with the two surgeons. The two surgeons would be back-to-back ... one surgeon facing toward my feet working on the abdomen correcting the hernia, while the other surgeon has his back to that surgeon while facing my head and working on the skull.

Because of their concern over my Sleep Apnea, I assume to be "safe", the anesthesiologist must have made an error on the side of too little anesthesia. I say that because I woke up in the middle of the operation and bolted straight up on the operating table. I will never forget the terror of seeing my scalp pulled down over my face with hair from my scalp covering my eyes. (What an extraordinary experience.) Both surgeons began screaming at the anesthesiologist, "Put him out!" "Put him out!" They pushed me back down flat on my back, and I quickly went back to sleep with additional anesthesia administered immediately. So, how did I get into this situation?

Two days earlier, I had been in the hospital for a hernia surgery that went well. I had been guilty of lifting too many heavy loads on our farm. They said I needed hernia surgery on both sides, but I had opted for only the worst side. I pleaded for the hospital not to release me because I did not feel strong enough to go home. The hospital, however, said I had to be out by noon in order for my insurance to cover me as "out-patient" surgery, or I would incur additional hospital costs at over $5,000 per day not covered under my insurance policy. Slightly before noon, the hospital discharged me, although I did not feel strong enough. I was wheeled out of the hospital in a wheelchair and driven home.

In the middle of the night, I passed out when I simply got up to walk to the bathroom. When I came to my senses, I knew something was wrong. I was lying on the bathroom floor. My wife was screaming. My daughter was screaming. My left eye was looking straight up normally, but my right eye was looking toward the sink cabinet to my right. My head was in excruciating pain. We later determined that I passed out while getting up in the middle of the night to go to the bathroom and I fell forward. I hit my forehead just above my right eye on the sharp marble corner of the ledge around the tub. The blow had crushed the right side of my skull behind my forehead and sent my right eye looking towards the right of my forehead. They called 911.

The emergency room gave me a CAT scan. Not only did my eye need plastic surgery to be put back into place, but also they would have to remove 128 shattered bone fragments out of my forehead because of hitting the marble corner of the tub ledge in the full force of falling when I passed out. They said they would then have to put a titanium plate screwed into the skull to cover up the open hole left by the broken skull. To save $5,000 for an extra day in the hospital was now going to cost the insurance company at least $50-60,000 additional to correct the accident.

I do not know what happened psychologically with that episode. I only know that when I recovered from surgery, I found that I became claustrophobic. I was never claustrophobic before. After that surgery, I could not stand to feel "closed in" by people on both sides in an auditorium, a movie theater, an aircraft, or in the back seat of an automobile or van. I had to be able to look out the front windshield of a car. I had to be able to lean over to see down the aircraft aisle for relief. I had to be able to look down the aisle of an auditorium in a movie or in church. From that time on, I had to have the aisle seat on flights, in theaters, church, movies, or any other event. If not, I would hyperventilate and have to leave or stand in the back. I could not be immobilized. Any situation where I could not move, like dental chairs, MRI's, Cat-scans, or X-rays caused extreme claustrophobia. That episode changed everything. One day I was okay ... the next day I was not. In order to sleep, I even had to change out my CPAP headgear with the nasal pillows to my nose coming from the side, instead of over the front of my face. It had even become claustrophobic to get to sleep.

I guess the trade-off is that while I struggle with this claustrophobic condition privately, the accidental by-product was a "face-lift" I received from the cranial surgery. The facelift is viewable by the public and positive. It helped me gain and retain jobs at an older age because of my appearance. Everyone thinks I

211

am much younger than I am. I would have had the same result if I had initiated and gone in for scheduled plastic surgery, like a facelift. The doctor said the way the surgery was done to get at the bone fragments, was similar to what is done frequently for a facelift. While the cosmetic surgeon had my scalp pulled down over my forehead to remove over 100 shattered bone fragments, he said he went ahead and scooped out some fatty deposits under my eyes, as he would do for a scheduled facelift, since he was already in there. Of course, they pulled the scalp back up over my forehead to put stitches across the top of my head from ear to ear and connected to the back part of my scalp. In doing that, they had to stretch the skin over my face to give them enough skin to connect across the top of my head. The doctor said the procedure gave me an unscheduled, unintended and unplanned "facelift." This unintended benefit has been such an asset. Most people guess my age as 10-15 years younger than I actually am. Fortunately, my energy level matches that impression of being younger.

While I experienced a catastrophic event during surgery, the surgery actually became a blessing over the years in terms of appearance. As you age, it is a blessing to appear younger than you really are. There is such a prejudice against age in the workforce today. Just when the grey hair comes, which in times past was an indication of age and wisdom of years lived, society wants to shelve you … to retire you. However, I have been able to utilize the wisdom that comes from my experience and age to do my job. I have not had any questioning perception of limitations my real age might bring because I look younger than I am in years. My energy and results back that up.

What was meant for bad, God turned around to be good. When you go through some things, you cannot help but wonder why God allows certain things to happen. It does not make sense when it happens. Nevertheless, that ordeal proved to be a blessing in my later years that I never could have anticipated. I am now so grateful today. The incredibly negative event proved to have an extraordinarily positive effect on my life.

*"For who knoweth what is good for man in this life..."* Ecclesiastes 6:12

*God does!*

# CRAZY RISKS

I was syndicating and raising money to buy an apartment complex in Indiana. It was 320 units in Muncie, Indiana, about 63 miles northeast of Indianapolis and the home of Ball State University, David Letterman's alma mater. In fact, Ball State is naming their new $21-million, Communications and Media Building after David Letterman. However, I digress.

I was selling shares and raising a couple of million dollars to renovate and rent a 320 unit apartment complex spread out on 47 acres. My Prospectus on the units had projections of Tax Deductions for the current year, but they were predicated on closing before December 31. In addition, I was $250,000 short of selling all the shares. If I didn't close before the end of the year, everyone who had already purchased shares and done their tax-planning based upon receiving those tax write-offs that year, could (and probably would) back out of the deal. I would lose those millions already invested, and I would have to start over selling shares the next year. Moreover, if I did not close by December 31, the seller could back out and demand my forfeiture of $50,000 earnest money. I would not only lose that, but I would have to begin all the legal work and security registrations again to revise the Prospectus, plus putting up more deposit money to get the seller to extend closing, if he would even do that. I had a couple of hundred thousand dollars at stake, and I did not have the money to buy the shares myself.

I contacted an investment advisor who had placed some of his clients in the deal, and told him of my dilemma. He gave me the contact number of one of his clients, who might loan me the money to close on $250,000 of shares in escrow, allowing me the time to try to sell them after the end of the year. What a risk. In addition, the collateral he wanted was for me to sign over the deed to my $1.2-million home to him to hold until I could pay him back in 30 days after I sold the additional shares. I stood to lose hundreds of thousands of dollars in real estate commissions, syndication fees, General Partner fees, more earnest money, and additional legal and security registration fees if I did not close. But if I borrowed the money to close and failed to sell the shares in escrow within 30-days, then I would end up owning a huge amount of shares that I borrowed $250,000 to buy, but had no way of paying back. I would be in debt, over leveraged, and I would lose my home.

Caught in a vise, I did it. I gave him my home as collateral for a 30-day, $250,000 loan. I flew to Indianapolis to close by December 31, on New Year's Eve. I was so nervous. I had not told my wife of the risk I was taking, and we were having a New Year's Party in our Cabin by the River behind our home. I closed and flew home to the New Year's Eve party, with knots in my stomach. I was going to be late anyway because of the flight, but my wife would be somewhat understanding of my being late to the party because she that when I closed, we would have received thousands of dollars in fees. She just did not know I had signed all of them away for a loan bigger than what I was to receive in fees after expenses and legal fees. In addition, if I could not resell the shares within 30-days, then I would have the liability of a huge ownership of shares of an apartment in Muncie, Indiana, plus the loss of our home. The time alone to think about this on the flight home to Atlanta felt like it was an eternity. Not only was I anxious about the risk I'd taken, but how I was going to tell my wife to be prepared for the possibility of having to pack up an 11,000 square foot home with nowhere to go. Could I even tell her?

I arrived late for the New Year's Eve party at my home in Atlanta, and I began greeting friends and neighbors. I never heard a word anyone said because I was so lost in stress. I could not even think about what people were saying to me. It was as if I was listening to their words, but they did not realize I was deaf ... I could not "hear" what they were saying. I was lost in thoughts about the "what ifs." I was under extraordinary pressure.

Within 30-days, I did sell out the $250,000 in shares and redeemed my home deed. Only then, did I tell my wife about the risk I had taken. She was justifiably upset, and I did not blame her. At that point, I determined that what I was risking was too much to continue to do deals, and that no amount of money was worth the knots in my stomach, the sleepless nights, and numb days. I needed to get off this treadmill of risk. The demand for these investments was slowing down.

An old Chinese Proverb says, "He who takes no risk deserves no gain." However, the risks had become too great. I needed to get out, and I did, involuntarily, because the government did it for me.

I designed and built an 11,000 square foot home on 32 acres in the Stone Mountain area of Atlanta. It included a 3,000 square foot office space in one wing.

# TAX REFORM ACT of 1986

*"Give me neither poverty nor riches ... Lest I be full, and deny thee, and say, 'Who is the Lord?' Or lest I be poor, and steal, and take the name of my God in vain."* Proverbs 30:8-9

What a bunch of stupid Congressmen! Did they not know they were going to wreak havoc on the real estate market? In 1983, Congress had liberalized tax deductions on real estate investments, even allowing aggressive component depreciation. General Partners began putting together large real estate deals, especially in apartments, to take advantage of the tax benefits for their clients due to the liberalized depreciation parameters in the 1983 law change. After everyone had been making real estate investments and taking write-offs based upon the criteria that Congress established in 1983, in 1986 Congress began to disallow the criteria and took the write-offs away, without grandfathering in those 1983 rules. Like a game of musical chairs, the music stopped. If you had invested based upon the 1983 laws, you were left standing in the game without being able to change in 1986, what you'd already committed to investment-wise. The tax deductions you were expecting that would provide a tax savings to fund the next payment, or multiple staged-in payments, was no longer going to be there because of the 1986 rule changes.

Suddenly, everyone was under-collateralized. The property values backed by real estate loans were collapsing. Without the value of the tax deductions established by earlier laws, this new set of 1986 rules was destroying values of commercial real estate ... especially apartments.

Primary lenders for apartment loans were the Savings and Loan associations. Suddenly, they were under-collateralized on

219

their loans, and thousands of S & L's went bankrupt. They did not have enough capital value and collateral backing the loans made to stay in business.

Therefore, this caused all but a few government employee or teacher's Savings and Loan entities to go out of business. Those of us who had syndicated large apartment projects to investors, especially using staggered multi-year funding for the equity part of the investment, found their investors no longer willing to make their next staged-in payment because the tax deductions no longer existed. While I do not blame the advice of the investors' attorneys and tax advisors to stop making additional investments in light of the law change which collapsed property values, that did nothing to help those of us who were General Partners on these deals, and I was one. As General Partner for those groups, I had only 5-10% ownership in each apartment syndication. However, I had 100% of the liability on the loans. Suddenly, I owed millions of dollars on apartment projects. Practically overnight, they had much less market value than the price at which they were purchased.

As General Partner, I had up to 35 individual Limited Partner investors in each apartment project syndication. The Limited Partners had Limited liability. I had General liability. Some wanted to stay in and make their continued obligated payments over the next few years, but most investors wanted to follow their tax and legal advisors and simply stop investing. They were told it would be putting "good money after bad." As it turned out later, based upon the congressionally induced price collapse, it was good advice. Therefore, I was left holding the bag on the loans, but without enough ownership or money to fund all of the additional payments required under the investment prospectus.

Since a few of the limited partners in each investment wanted to continue, and because I wanted to do the right thing by all of the investors, I put the Limited Partnerships that owned the apartments in Chapter 11 Bankruptcy Reorganization. We restructured the deals, liabilities, loan documents, and subsequent payments. New agreements were sent to the limited partners for signature through the bankruptcy court to continue the investment under the new terms. If any investors elected not to continue his or her share, then another investor who wanted to stay in would have to pick up that abandoned share in addition to their initial share. Many in each group did not want to continue, even after the renegotiated terms. Those wanting to stay in at their current level could not fund the additional level of obligation of those who wanted to drop out. Under that scenario, it was impossible to continue. Each Partnership converted from a Chapter 11 Reorganization, to a Chapter 7 Liquidation in the Courts.

The apartments sold at huge discounts and everyone lost their invested money. In addition, the cancellation of debt on the loans as the properties liquidated were imputed to the investors as "gains" because the loans were part of the basis of the value upon which tax deductions were based. This meant that not only did investors lose their cash investment made, but they incurred a tax liability for the "paper" gains imputed due to loan forgiveness and write-offs taken. This is called "Phantom Income;" revenue that is reported to the Internal Revenue Service as income gains for tax purposes but is not actually received by the individual purportedly receiving it. Taxes are owed on Phantom Income, "paper revenue," due to the structure of the investment.

Although I had 100% of the loan liabilities as General Partner, I had no personal liability on the loans. Due to good counsel from

Larry Burkett, I negotiated the loans to be fully exculpated loans. In other words, there was no personal liability to pay them back, because the property itself stood for the full value collateralizing the property loans. However, I did have the Phantom Revenue "gains" from the forgiveness of the loans in bankruptcy. The result ... I owed the IRS over a million dollars for the Phantom Revenues "gained" on paper from the millions of dollars in debt forgiveness ... revenues I had "gained" on paper, not "earned" or "received," but taxable Phantom "income," nevertheless. There is no way to win with the IRS, regardless of how conservatively you structure your deals.

There I was. I lost all my investments right along with my partners' losses. I lost the potential gains from expected profits before the law changed: I lost my investors; my management revenues from property management; the anticipated real estate commissions on the expected sales in the future; and, I had to report millions of dollars in phantom revenues from the debt forgiveness and write-offs taken and recaptured. Losing all the above, I now owed the IRS $1.2 million in taxes for the phantom income reported on paper, but not earned in cash. There was no way I could ever pay back over a million dollars the IRS said I owed on these phantom revenues. Somehow, I simply had to trust God to work all of this out ... someday. Financially wiped out, I was no longer a multi-millionaire. I had nowhere else to turn to except God.

The sad thing is that before the Tax Reform Act of 1986, I had never returned less than 100% annual profit to investors for each year of their investment. Congress killed a very profitable business venture and wiped out millions of investors, along with the entire Savings & Loan industry. In one book, I read that the aggregate years of business experience for those Congressional committees creating the law was seven (7) years ... that is a total among all of them. On the other hand, the combined political experience was in the hundreds of years.

We need businessmen in Congress who understand the free enterprise system and the cause and effect of business from the "ideas" they pass into law. Knowing more about politics than business, they certainly created an extraordinary, devastating life change for me ... from multi-millionaire to pauper; plus owing over a million dollars in taxes on phantom income not received as spendable income. In one lack-of-understanding vote, Congress collapsed the S & L's, apartment real estate, the asset values of thousands of investors, and me. The negative results from the elected Congressmen's lack of business sense and understanding were extraordinary.

# HOUSE AUCTION

*"And the borrower is servant to the lender."* Proverbs 22:7

The crowd gathered in front of my house on auction day was much smaller than I expected ... and smaller than the auctioneers predicted. To attract a crowd, the Auctioneers even advertised "opening bid" as $100,000 on a $1.5 million home. The bank was going to take it if I had not placed it up for sale. I only owed $300,000 on it ... less than 20% of its construction value. I had $1.2 million in equity in the house. I had been conservative and built it for cash out of pocket over several years. When the real estate market turned down, even though I had built the home for cash to almost completion over five years with $1.2 million after-tax dollars, I became impatient. I finally took out a signature loan and borrowed that last $300,000 to complete construction.

I listed the house for sale years earlier, but the realtors said I needed to finish all construction before I could expect a serious offer or any real efforts to sell it. The Realtors said it was difficult for prospective buyers to visualize what it would look like upon completion. They also said, "Anyone buying a house this expensive would not want to have to engage in further construction." After having it listed for five years, and constantly lowering the price, it still did not sell. In addition, because my own business was slacking off, the bank called my $300,000 signature loan, even though I was *fully current* with the interest-only payments on the loan. "At least I might be able to pay the bank loan plus recover some of my money invested in the house as a result of the auction," I thought.

Embarrassingly enough, there were a lot of friends and neighbors there to witness my misery. The vultures were hoping for a steal of a deal. This was "everyone vs. me." I was trying to get enough of my equity back out of the auction to start over in a smaller home, debt free.

The vultures won. Not only was there not enough bid to cover the $300,000 loan, but there was not enough to gain back any of my $1.2 million hard-earned equity invested in the house. What a nightmare. The bank made me offer the adjacent 12 acres for auction that had a deep-water well and a lake. It also went to a bidder for a steal.

A bigger nightmare ... Still not enough to cover the $300,000 owed to the bank. The bank had the auctioneer begin to go through the house to auction off our furnishings. Now, the crowd of buyers really smelled blood: Final bid on the $11,000, 12-ft. long, dining room table - $300;  An almost new washer and dryer - $5 each; A beautiful wrought iron patio set - $20; and so on. The blood bath continued until the bank got enough above the auctioneer's fee to satisfy the bank's $300,000 signature loan. Everything I had labored and worked for all these years was gone.

I was sick to my stomach. It was like a nightmare slowly playing out before me ... and all my neighbors. I ran into one of the bathrooms, knelt before the ceramic throne, and began throwing up. I had never before experienced vomiting violently from upset nerves instead of from a physical illness.

I was glad my wife had flown to my brothers' house in Chicago to avoid this pain. I do not know if she had a premonition of what was going to happen. Perhaps she merely knew she could not endure the pressure of witnessing the possible debacle. She was already fighting cancer. This stress would have certainly taken her earlier than the cancer did. I was healthy, and this felt like it was killing me. I dreaded calling and telling my wife. Not only were the bids not enough to have a surplus above the note to start over again on a smaller scale, but we were wiped out. The house was gone. The adjacent 12-acre lake property was gone, too, as well as some of her furniture and antiques, all for cents on the dollar.

When Proverbs says, *"The borrower is servant to the lender,"* I got it. You do not have to explain it to me. I got it! In fact, I have lived through the horrors of the lesson with that scripture written by Solomon. Scripture says that Solomon was the richest man to have ever lived, and he was the wisest. As I read the Proverbs, I often wonder how it came about that God placed such wisdom into Solomon. His Proverbs hold true thousands of years after they were written. What a hard lesson to learn … *"The borrower IS servant to the lender."* I would not wish this extraordinary, painful experience on anyone.

# HOSPICE

*"To everything, there is a season, and a time to every purpose under the heaven: A time to be born, and a time to die."* Ecclesiastes 3:1-2

Not yet 55 years old, it was just too early to give up someone as incredible as my wife was. Bertie's breast cancer had turned me into a full-time caregiver, which kept me busy and optimistic. We both thought she would "win." Everyone always thinks that they will "beat it." *Remission* ... it is an elusive, almost magical word we lived to hear after each test, doctor visit or chemotherapy treatment. However, we never did.

It was a real shock when the deterioration set in so quickly. A sudden decision was made to release her from the hospital. I moved a hospital bed into our home with a hospice nurse assigned, and I moved Bertie into our master bedroom. I moved everything back against the walls to make room for the large hospital bed. Not even 24 hours had passed since her release from Emory University Hospital in Atlanta, early the next morning she was gone! I was numb. Everything happened so fast. At that time in my life, I thought Hospice was simply home-care nursing. I had no idea of the gravity of the situation when someone became under the care of Hospice. Since then, I have learned from studying that as far back as the 11th century, transferring to Hospice care meant that the doctors have determined someone to be terminally ill. However, during my wife's battle, I was completely unaware that I should have expected to have no hope of Bertie's survival once Hospice became involved.

I should have known. The doctors at Emory Hospital were very kind, and encouraged me to be optimistic. I remember one day they came for her and wheeled her down the hall for another test.

Bertie had been having such trouble catching her breath, even in a resting state. She was only happy when a huge fan sitting on the dresser close to her bed was set on "high" and pointing in her face. The wind blowing in her face made her *feel* like she was getting enough air to breathe. We became aware that we dared not walk between her and the high force of air from the fan to her face, because she would panic. Cutting off that breeze made her feel that she was not getting enough air to breathe. Eventually, we found out that her lung surfaces were giving her very little healthy cell surface to assimilate oxygen.

The hospital staff came for Bertie and wheeled her out and down the hall for a procedure. The procedure put her "out" and dropped a camera down her air passages into her lungs. The pictures they took were very scary. In color, they pointed out that the only places usable to assimilate oxygen were in "red" (the "good" cells). The area of black cells in her lungs simply could not get air to her. The "red" areas were less than 15% of the total interior lung-wall area, no matter which side of her lung you were observing from the photographs. I became sick in the pit of my stomach to see to how much the spread of cancer had destroyed her interior lung surface. No wonder she had to have the psychological (and maybe even the physical) help of the fan blowing in her face to survive trying to breathe. Still, I was hopeful. The doctors were doing everything modern medicine had trained them to do.

I will never forget the afternoon after that last test. A young intern took me around the corner of the hallway and asked me if "I was aware of what's really going on?" He said, "Your wife is dying ... she probably has two weeks or less to live." Again, I was stunned. *"He's only a new intern,"* I thought, *"and the seasoned doctors are doing everything they can for her. Besides, they've never told me anything like that ... not even remotely like that."* I know you have to be optimistic to survive, but I suddenly felt like I was being unrealistically deceptive to myself. This was the first time I had ever entertained the idea that Bertie might not "make it." Wow! A shocking dose of reality flooded my brain. My first thought was, *"I don't think I can make it without her."* Next, I thought, *"Does she know? Does she think that she is dying and is simply not telling me? Have the doctors told her, and she won't let them tell me to keep from discouraging me?"*

The next call in the hospital room was for me to go down to the Hospice Office on the first floor of the Hospital. They told me Bertie was going to be released and sent home today. The doctors could do nothing more for her. *The Intern was right!* They said a Hospice nurse would check in on us frequently. I responded that I was in no way able to have her go home that afternoon, and that I needed time and help to prepare for her to come home. They said they would delay her release another day, which would give Hospice time to deliver a hospital bed to our home. Then, the ambulance would transport her to our home the following day.

All of that happened the next day. The Hospice nurse was there within an hour to administer morphine for her pain. Bertie was very sensitive and the morphine made her sick.

At 2:00 am the next morning, my brother's wife, Margaret, came downstairs to the couch where I was sleeping. She woke me and simply said, "Dean, she's Gone." I jumped up and ran up the flight of stairs, taking 2 to 3 steps at a time and burst into our bedroom. There, I saw Bertie frozen stiff, in a half-pulled up position with both hands on one side of the hospital bed rails as

231

she tried to pull herself up. Her mouth was stuck open in a gasping-for-air maneuver; a sight that will never be erased from my memory ... *Never!* What was I going to do without my Bertie?

This experience had an extraordinary effect on me. I used to jog 5-miles per day, 5 days per week. After that event, even my slightest beginning to breathe hard or needing air would slam that image in my mind, and I backed off until I could regain my breath. If I did not, I would feel like I was losing my mind and control of my being. My mind would go crazy. I could not stand to get out of breath or to breathe hard. I always pulled back to catch my breath. I just could not deal with that image in my mind of Bertie trying to gasp for her last breath. Anytime I got out of breath, that image of Bertie popped into my brain, and I would back off until I was breathing normally. This condition has led me to a very sedentary lifestyle that I fight to this very day.

I do not have any good images when the word "Hospice" is used. I am grateful for those who serve in hospice. It is a very tough job to do, and someone has to have the heart to do it. I just cannot imagine dealing with the Hospice situations as a job to do regularly. It is extraordinary how they lovingly preside over death. God bless those people who can be caregivers when it is *"a time to die."*

# GEORGIA HOUSE of REPRESENTATIVES
# BILL HR 36EX
# Aug. 25, 1995

*"Who can find a virtuous woman? For her price
is far above rubies." Proverbs 31:10*

It is still hard for me to know how my first wife, Bertie, could be a stay-at-home wife, and yet make such an impact on the world. Literally, hundreds of people came to her funeral from 30 different states. The funeral home chapel only sat 320 people. So many people showed up that we had to move the funeral to a nearby church gymnasium. There simply was not enough room to hold all the people who had traveled across country from dozens of states to see and hear the last remarks about her and pay their respects to her. I still don't know how a housewife, who never taught a Sunday school class, never did radio or TV, never wrote an article, never wrote a book, never made speeches, was never in the public eye or never promoted herself in any way could possibly become well-known enough to draw that many people to her funeral. I was always out doing business, speaking, and transacting business deals, while Bertie stayed at home, full time, for our two daughters, Catherine and Christine, and as my support.

Of course, I knew that when she did accompany me on business trips, she always drew everyone to her, so that everyone who ever met Bertie would refer to her as "my best friend," even after just one meeting. Yep ... they all said that. She was so genuinely interested in everyone she met and they were made to feel that they were her very "best friend."

While on the way to the bank on the day she died, I was shocked when I heard the talk on the radio. Certain politicians, radio hosts, and others on local talk shows in Atlanta were speaking of Bertie's death and saying how all of Atlanta would miss her. One politician remarked that he was going to introduce a bill to designate the next day, "Bertie Webb Day"... and he did introduce a Resolution.

For this book, I entered a search on Google for "Georgia House of Representatives, Bertie Webb Day", and I found the bill; "Georgia House of Representatives Bill HR 36EX," expressing regret at the passing of Bertie that had been introduced the day after she died by Georgia House Representative, Ronald A. Crews. It was introduced in the Georgia House of Representatives and read on 8/25/1995, and it passed the first time as "Georgia House of Representatives bill HR 36EX – Bertie Rigdon Webb; condolences."

The bill read:

# A RESOLUTION

Expressing regret at the passing of Ms. Bertie Rigdon Webb; and for other purposes:

WHEREAS, Ms. Bertie Rigdon Webb, beloved wife and mother, passed away on August 24, 1995, at the untimely age of 53 years; and

WHEREAS, she was born on October 24, 1940, the daughter of Robert and Ethel Rigdon, and she was the wife of Dean Oliver Webb, the mother of Catherine and Christine, and the "adopted mother" of Ansley; and

WHEREAS, Bertie was a child of God who devoted her life to her Lord and Savior Jesus Christ; and

WHEREAS, she lived her faith each and every day and exuded a joy of living that was an inspiration to everyone she met, and all who knew her counted her as a friend and respected her integrity and her humor; and

WHEREAS, she loved her country and actively participated in the political process to better her county state and nation; and

WHEREAS, while Bertie will be sorely missed by her family and her many friends, we will take comfort in the absolute knowledge that she is now celebrating life in the presence of the One she loved the most.

NOW THEREFORE, BE IT RESOLVED BY THE HOUSE of REPRESENTATIVES that the members of this body express regret at the passing of Ms. Bertie Rigdon Webb and convey sincere condolences to her family and friends.

BE IT FURTHER RESOLVED, that the Clerk of the House of Representatives is authorized and directed to transmit an appropriate copy of this Resolution to the family of Ms. Bertie Rigdon Webb.

Office of the Clerk of the House

Robert E. Rivers, Jr., Clerk of the House

*"Who can find a virtuous woman? Her price is far above rubies, and she shall be praised."* Even as a loving housewife and mother, she found a way to impact others so much that they simply had to get their condolences in a Bill to memorialize her in the permanent, Official Records in the State House of Georgia Capitol.

A virtuous woman indeed ... Obviously, I was blessed to be married to such an extraordinary woman.

# FUNERAL

*"But a woman that feareth the Lord, she shall be praised."* Proverbs 31:30

"Where are you going to have the funeral services?" Dr. Crist asked me. "Well, here in the funeral home chapel," I replied. My friend, Dr. Johnny Crist, Pastor of The Vineyard Churches in Atlanta, whispered to me that they were already on the second guest book, and there were entries from 30 states. He told me that the funeral home chapel with a 320 seating capacity was simply not going to hold everyone. He said it appeared that there could be over 1,000 people at the funeral tomorrow. I needed to do something, and do it quickly. I was in such grief that I could not even think. "Can you do something?" I asked him. He said if I would trust him, he would take charge over everything and make all the changes and arrangements necessary to make it work. That was so very good, and a great relief, because I was in too much grief, and too dazed to think clearly.

"Dr. John", as I affectionately called him, did take over. Dr. Johnny Crist told the funeral home we were not going to use the chapel tomorrow … the funeral would be held in a different location with a larger room and more seating. Tomorrow was a Sunday, and the funeral was not until 3:00 PM, long after all church services would be over. He still had difficulty securing adequate room nearby the funeral home. However, he was successful in arranging for the use of a church gymnasium only a mile away. He had someone draw up a simple map from the funeral home to the church gym down the street. After church, he had his men located at each entrance of the funeral home parking lot entrances to hand out the map with the simple directions to the new location; a church one mile south of the funeral home. Dr. Crist's men from

237

the church verbally told all car occupants that the venue had been changed because of insufficient seating. There was a massive line of autos waiting to turn into the funeral home parking lot. One-by-one, they received a map and verbal instructions about the venue change. They made U-turns through the funeral home parking lot and headed south in the direction of the church on the hand-drawn map. What were we all doing here? No one could believe that Bertie was dead.

There we were with hundreds of people coming from dozens of states to pay their respects to this "housewife" we all loved so much. Each one of us felt that Bertie was our very best friend. I guess we all thought Bertie considered us her "very best friend." She made everyone feel that way, whether or not one knew her for years or just met her for the first time.

Over 1,000 people assembled from 30-states in a church gymnasium to pay respects to Bertie, who was dearly loved by all who met her. It was late. After all, everyone came to a funeral scheduled to start at 3:00pm, but had to turn around and follow a map to another location a mile away. Late or not, we started. A letter of tribute was read from the CBN Board member, Harold Bredesen. The Garth Brooks recorded song, *If tomorrow never comes,"* that Dean sang to Bertie was played. The open mic allowed many to express what Bertie meant to them. It was a poignant, but powerful, memorable time ... a celebration and tribute to an extraordinary life. Bertie never taught a Sunday school class and never spoke publically or did a seminar. She was never on the radio, never wrote a book and never did anything publically. She simply prayed, stayed in the Word and loved on people. Yet, here were over 1,000 people from 30 states convened on a Sunday to pay tribute to this one life and the impact she had on them. It was an extraordinary event. As Proverbs 31:30 says, *"A woman that feareth the Lord, she shall be praised."*

**Bertie**

# GRIEVING

*"But though he cause grief, yet will he have compassion according to the multitude of his mercies."* Lamentation 3:32

I curled up in a fetal position. My wife of over 32 years passed away after a two-year battle with breast cancer, and I felt lost. She was the love of my life, and I felt like a piece of me was gone forever. I did not care to go on. I did not care about my future. I did not care about any goals, work ... anything. I just simply did not care to live.

The pain of my life was just too overwhelming to bear. I had to escape. I fell asleep late every night, at least the nights that I could even get to sleep. I usually woke up just before noon or so, and after several cups of coffee, I drove to a theatre to see a noontime movie ... a different movie every day at a different theater every day. That was my escape from the thoughts of my reality, mental pain and misery. I escaped the thoughts of despair in my mind by medicating with attention to another's story on the screen. I went to so many movies, I barely stayed ahead of the new releases, and Atlanta is a huge city with many movie theaters. I chose to live every day's existence through another person's story on the screen in a sea of forgetfulness and mental diversion. I am so glad I did not drink or do drugs. No telling where I would be today if that had ever been in my life.

One day, I bumped into an old friend. To this day, I do not even remember who it was because my mind was in a fog. I remember dumping my pain on him, and I do remember the advice he gave me. He suggested that I call every man I knew to ask them for a referral of someone they knew who had been married at least 25 years or more, and had lost their wife in death. He told me to ask them how they dealt with their grief when their wife passed away. While there was some overlap, each one had a specific thing that was more helpful to them than any other. Therefore, I wrote their best advice down and began my period of taking steps to initiate "proactive" grieving ... no longer just "zoning out," but actually taking steps to facilitate dealing with my grief.

Following the first man's suggestion, I gathered all the pictures I had of my deceased wife, Bertie, including those I had in storage. The process included going back to her baby pictures. The pictures included those of her growing up, her college days, our wedding, the births of our daughters, travel to Europe ... all complete pictorial evidence of fun during our 32 years of marriage. I spread them all out on the floor. Through buckets of tears, I began to place the pictures in chronological order. That took a couple of weeks. I cannot tell you how many times I had to wipe my fallen tears off a picture lying on the floor as I spread them out to arrange them chronologically through her life.

I then purchased a huge 3-ring binder with plastic inserts and began documenting the chronological life of my deceased wife in pictures. It was a gut-wrenching experience but very healing. I was able to live out her whole life in pictures, recalling our college days when we met, to my Navy absences in Vietnam, the birth of our two daughters, our family trips to Europe, Canada and out west to Yellowstone Park. I was able to give thanks for a lifetime of glorious, memorable experiences with her that some marriages never get to experience. As I finally thumbed through that pictorial album, I was able to weep, and I thanked God for each experience I had with her ... memories of all the many good times shared.

The advice I followed from the next referral was also very healing. I followed the suggestion exactly how he said he did it when his wife died. He said it would help bring closure to our life. Therefore, according to his instructions, I wrote out a "goodbye" love letter to my deceased wife, Bertie. I then propped up a large, framed 11x14 picture of her on the fireplace mantle so it would be eye level. Then, I read my goodbye-love letter to her face in the photo. I told her how much she meant to me. I read about how much she gave to me during our lives together. I then ceremoniously removed my wedding ring and held it up to her. I told her I was removing our ring to symbolize the end of our life together. I described to her picture how I woke up in my fetal position ... every morning, always crying, just in case she had not seen it from heaven. Even though I had always told Bertie that I would never remarry if something happened to her, my mind was changing. I told her picture that after four months of grieving, the thought came to me that I was "too good to waste." I told her I would probably remarry again. She was the most wonderful thing that had ever happened to me, but I had to move on. I knew how to respect and love a woman, so I should remarry. I was now hoping to find happiness with another for the balance of my life. However, I told her that doing this would not diminish the memories of the life we had together in any way ... she would never be forgotten. In fact, I told her that the reason I could even consider remarrying was that my experience of marriage was so extremely wonderful ... that I wanted continue to have more loving experiences with someone else. In reality, it was the good times we shared together that only made me want more. I guess this ceremony was giving me permission to think and explore the possibility of another marriage. This "Goodbye and Ring Removal Ceremony" was giving myself permission to consider another

243

relationship in the future. I had a twinge that felt like I was betraying my wife ... cheating on her, because we were so close and connected. However, I knew this was a necessary step in the healing process and moving on.

I was very surprised when I exposed my marital feelings to some of the men in our church. It was evident that they viewed my situation much differently than I did. Men in our church said things to me like: "Wow, now you're free to do whatever you want, with no recourse;" and "You're free as a bird to do whatever you want;" or "I wish I could have your freedom." I did not like my freedom! I was plumbed and wired to be faithfully married and could only hope that I could be married again someday. It never entered my mind that I was free to go wild now. I was surprised and shocked as they shared their perspective of my situation with me.

The fact that I was proactive in aggressively pursuing actions to help me get through the grieving process was of immense benefit. I guess I could have spent more time in bed, going to movies and other activities while trying to forget and numb the pain. The time I spent following the advice of those men who had shared their experience dealing with their losses was the best, well-spent time ever. If this ever happens to you, I highly recommend being aggressive in dealing with your grief.

Someone told me that men who lose their mate grieve for a shorter time than women who lose their mate. As time goes on, my observation is that this appears to be true. However, I cannot over-emphasize how important it is to be proactive in dealing with your grief. It still hurts. Sometimes you do not want to go on with life. Aggressively going after memories, being thankful for the years you had, and not concentrating on how short life can be is a very healing thing to do. I recommend it to all widowers. I thank God for allowing and directing me to an unbelievable mate in marriage that I cherished sharing life with for over three decades. Every man should be so blessed. Life with Bertie was extraordinary.

# OFFER-IN-COMPROMISE MIRACLE

*"He is a debtor to the whole law."* Galatians 5:3b

How could I possibly owe the IRS over a million dollars? How could I owe taxes on money I never received in cash or payments of any kind? Oh, Yes! *That is* why they call it *"Phantom Income."*

I had syndicated hundreds of apartments in Georgia, South Carolina and Indiana. As General Partner, I sold shares to limited partners. As General Partner, even though I only had a maximum of a 5-10% ownership in the partnerships, I had 100% of the liability and obligation on the loans I structured for the Limited Partnerships. I never returned less than 100% profit per year, cash-on-cash returns to the limited partners on the liquidated partnerships. For those of you who understand IRR, Internal Rates of Return, from a tax standpoint, the IRR's were over 200-400%, and even 3,000% on one partnership. People would fight to get into my deals. My attorney had to line up the applications and go by the postal time-stamp to determine who was first in line for the shares offered for investment.

When Congress passed the Tax Reform Act of 1986 and Ronald Reagan signed it into law, the entire real estate tax-incentive structure investments in the market collapsed in value, especially apartments. The Act did not grandfather in the 1983 Tax Act that liberalized tax incentives, such as accelerated component depreciation. Therefore, it unraveled and negated incentives for those already in deals purchased with those tax benefits incentivized in 1983. Consequently, almost every syndicated apartment deal was instantly under water on value when compared to its mortgage. Investors with staged-in payments over

5 years, for example, were advised by their attorneys and CPAs to stop their next obligated payments because they felt that everything would collapse, and additional payments would only be "good money after bad." This means they would lose their investment to date ... but no more. When the music stopped, there was no chair for the General Partner to sit on. I was the one left holding the properties with 100% obligation for the loans. My attorney advised me to place all the properties into Chapter 11 Bankruptcy Reorganization to be fair to investors in each syndication who did not want to bail out, but wanted to stay in the investment through a restructuring of the deal.

Therefore, I did. However, when the total of the next staged payments were divided by the smaller number of investors wanting to remain in, the next staged payments were so high for each that they could not even afford to stay in themselves, and they dropped out also. So there I was ... holding hundreds of apartment units in limited partnerships all by myself, with no way to pay everyone's share by myself. I had to convert the Chapter 11 reorganization bankruptcies into Chapter 7 liquidation bankruptcies. All of those apartments were foreclosed upon.

Fortunately, I had listened to the advice of my friend, Larry Burkett, Founder of Christian Financial Concepts, Inc. I demanded exculpatory language on the loans. Exculpation meant that I was not personally liable or responsible for any deficiencies between the loan amounts and the current market value of the properties. This was good because the Tax Reform Act of 1986 had instantly collapsed values to below the mortgage amounts. In fact, that Act wiped out the whole Savings and Loan (S & L) industry. There used to be an S & L on most every street. Now, they are rare. Every property with an S & L loan instantly became under collateralized because of the Tax Reform Act of 1986.

However, exculpation for deficiencies in values under loans did not waive the obligation on the mortgages. In Chapter 7 liquidation and foreclosure, all of that debt became debt forgiveness, which became income to me … "phantom income" on my tax return filings. Under IRS tax rules, although I never received the remuneration in cash as General Partner, the taxes I owed was on paper. This meant I suddenly owed over a million dollars, and I had received no income with which to pay the taxes, nor had I received any income on which the taxes were based. Since I lost the management contracts on those foreclosed properties I was managing, I also suddenly had no monthly management income at all.

I struggled to survive. Any income I received from consulting work, I had to have paid to me in cash. I put it on my tax returns and paid taxes on it. I learned that the IRS immediately seized any funds deposited in the bank, and if I kept my bank balance under $100, they left it alone. If the balance went over $100, the IRS seized it. Therefore, in order to survive, I never let the balance go over $100.

I lived for the next 14 years using cash and money orders to pay bills and income taxes. When I walked up to the service desk at my local Kroger grocery store, I was greeted with, "Hello, Mr. Webb. Are you here to pay your utility bills?" That was my monthly routine. Eventually, I borrowed $30,000 from an Alabama bank and made an Offer-in-Compromise settlement offer to the IRS. After 14 years of living on cash and settling bills and taxes with purchased money orders, the IRS settled for cents on the dollar. I had nothing left for them to take, so they accepted the compromise offer of the loan proceeds.

Once I signed the settlement, I was suddenly like a real person again. I could get a job, deposit payroll checks, use a checking account, and begin paying off the loan I obtained to make the settlement offer to the IRS.

I had mixed emotions. On the one hand, I was upset by the fact that I owed over a million dollars on phantom income I never received. Conversely, it was an absolute miracle to be able to settle that debt for less than 3-cents on the dollar of what they said I "owed," including fees, penalties, and accrued interest. To me, that was extraordinary. But, even though I don't agree with the Phantom Income rules, whereby you can owe taxes on money never earned, Galatians 5:3b says: *"... he is a debtor to the whole law,"* and, that I was!

# THE CHALLENGE

*"But the righteous are bold as a lion.* Proverbs 28:1

Who was I to challenge the Georgia political party's slate of elected delegates to the 1996 National Convention in San Diego? The convention chair gaveled the thousands of delegates to be quiet so he could read the slate of their proposed delegates from that convention's election committee. The noise of chatter lowered to a muffled din as he read the slate of selected delegates selected by the Convention Nominating Committee. Upon completion, the Chairman asked if there were any challenges from the floor for any of the selected seats. I had gone through the application process and been interviewed by them, but not selected as a delegate on their nomination slate to present at the convention.

The convention grew quiet because, of course, no one would dare challenge the selected nominations of the convention's Nomination Committee and even hope to sway the vote of thousands of delegates. The chair recognized the *gentleman at microphone four* who spoke, "I would like to place in nomination, Dean Webb, to challenge seat number nine." The crowd got loud again when the conversations broke out after seeing the name in the number nine slot of the list of 48 nominated delegates.

I overheard, "Who is Dean Webb? Does he know what he is doing? He's challenging someone who gives a million dollars to the party"... and other things, even personal attacks too nasty to put into writing.

A month earlier, I had gone before the Nomination Committee at my District Convention. I was not selected for consideration as a delegate. Earlier this same day, I had gone before the Nomination

251

Committee of this State Convention and, again, was not selected to be on the slate to be voted upon by the convention delegates. I suppose that the memories of 1988 were still fresh where I bucked the party insiders to back Pat Robertson. I was now bucking them from the floor of the State Convention. How dare I?

While the vote was taken moments earlier to elect the nominations committees' recommended slate of delegates, I approached a man who just lost the floor battle for the convention's vote to be the new party chairperson. In politics, name recognition is everything. I asked that he first identify himself by saying his name when called to the floor microphone and *then* place my name in nomination against the name in position nine of the slate. Since name recognition is critical in politics, I figured his name would carry some weight when he made a challenge nomination. I figured no one really knew the name of the person in slot number nine, who was a behind-the-scenes donor. She was not active in the party, and they were trying to "reward" her with a national delegate slot in appreciation for her party financial sponsorship. It was a calculated gamble. I hoped I targeted the right delegate to challenge. Additionally, since 1988, Georgia had voted heavily Republican. Therefore, the state had picked up another eight national delegate slots; 48 in 1996 instead of the 40 allowed in 1988.

After the shock of someone daring to challenge the "wisdom" of the whole convention nomination committee's elected slate, the chair proposed giving candidates three minutes on stage at the podium before polling the convention for their votes on the challenged position. They let the delegate selected by the Nominations Committee go first. While she spoke, the party officers and others took me aside and did verbal, angry onslaughts against me, trying to get my withdrawal. I refused to withdraw before the convention vote.

She thought she was a shoe-in, since her nomination came through the Convention's Committee. She was completely unprepared for a speech, and it showed. On the other hand, in the event the State nomination committee turned me down, I had prepared as I had at the District level. I rehearsed a three-minute speech that was powerful. In fact, I typed out a five-minute speech, but color-coded the paragraph sections to remove in case I was only allotted three minutes in a run-off. I used the three-minute version.

When they polled the whole convention, District by District, I won. It was a calculated, gutsy move, but it worked. I was elected as one of Georgia's 48 delegates to the 1996 Republican National Convention in San Diego. My courage to do a gutsy convention challenge paid off. Proverbs 28:1 says, *"The righteous are as bold as a lion."* What a memory and an extraordinary experience.

A collage of favorite moments from being an elected delegate to the 1996 Republican National Convention, which hangs on my office wall.

# THE 1996 SAN DIEGO NATIONAL CONVENTION

The convention center floor was crammed with elected delegates wearing Bob Dole hats and blowing horns. In spite of all the noise, trumped up energy and excitement it felt dead and contrived. Underneath it all was a foreboding feeling. We were going through the motions for the cameras. However, behind closed doors, many of the delegates talked about this convention, referring to the Republican Party's future, as disappointing ... at least for this election. Compared to the 1988 Convention in New Orleans, with competing candidates for their party's nomination, this felt dead. It was not an open convention ... no competition or mystery. I could not find anyone who actually thought Bob Dole "would" win ... just that he "could" win, if everything went right ... if Bill Clinton should stumble as the Democratic Party's nominee. In the midst of the festivities on the convention floor, it felt depressing to me. The excitement felt superficial, contrived and ingenuine. The horns blew out of party obligation for the TV cameras and not out of excitement for the candidate.

Senator Bob Dole spent the previous years traveling to do speeches for various local candidates around the U.S. In the process, he asked for support and received the word of many party leaders and insiders that they would commit to support him as the Presidential nominee. He was smart to gain those earlier pledges. When other more viable candidates might emerge later, Dole already had the verbal commitment of party and state leaders around the Country. He had their support locked in. Smart!

I also attended the 1988 convention in New Orleans as a delegate. Like before, I was allowed one guest, and I took my daughter Christy. I recall that the best party event invitation was a breakfast hosted by a Senator. We boarded a huge yacht and went up and down the coast of San Diego. We listened to speeches while being served a sumptuous breakfast by formal, white-gloved waiters. Mostly, I remember the wonderful weather, food, waiters and coastline. I do not remember any of the speeches. I do not even remember the Senator who made the invite. Since our presidential candidate did not win, I was not going to the inauguration festivities the next year. Therefore, it was just an uneventful trip to San Diego. Politically, it was an exercise in futility. However, the weather was nice.

Honestly, out of the millions of people who cast votes for the Presidential candidate of their choice every four years, it is a rare honor and a memorable experience to be elected as one of your state's few delegates to the National Convention ... I was one of the fortunate 48 in the state of Georgia.

Regardless of the outcome, very few are ever able to participate in an extraordinary experience like this one ... being an elected delegate to a National Convention.

# BURNED COLLATERAL

The picture and headlines in the paper turned my stomach. I was walking through the Atlanta airport to get my luggage, when I spotted a news headline regarding a pizza warehouse destroyed by fire. Just two days earlier, prior to my trip to visit my mother in Tulsa, I accepted the warehouse as collateral on a million dollar judgment awarded to me by a jury for fraud committed against me. I was in court for seven years trying to get justice for the fraud committed against me financially. The defendants hid all their assets. The only way the attorneys believed I had a chance of collecting on my fraud judgment was to attach any of their tangible assets, if we could find them. The only asset we could find was the warehouse from which they shipped pizza dough and toppings to their franchised pizza restaurants. My attorney legally attached that warehouse. Unable to get out of that, they provided a legal document. I signed it and received the warehouse as full collateral for the million-dollar judgment for fraud. I recognized the warehouse that was now "mine" in the newspaper headline photos of the fire. It burned to the ground.

We learned about their shady, previous dealings in other states during the discovery part of trial preparation. I just knew, immediately, that they got even with me by torching my only collateral against their judgment. I was sick. It had only been two days since I signed the agreement accepting the warehouse as settlement for the million-dollar fraud judgment. I knew I would never be able to collect cash. I thought I had a chance to get at least some of my money back on operating or selling the warehouse. Now, that was gone. Not only was the money to pay me back on the investment losses gone, but also the punitive damages awarded to me by the jury for the fraud was gone.

Almost two years before I purchased the pizza franchises, I had sensed the fallout from the Tax Reform Act of 1986 was going to devastate the real estate market, which it did. Therefore, I began looking for ways to diversify my investments while I still had income. I invested $650,000 in five pizza franchise locations; three existing stores, and two new areas to expand with two more franchised stores in the future. As soon as I took over the operations of the existing three stores, I realized they misrepresented sales and profits. The numbers were nowhere near as large as they represented when they sold to me. They were keeping two sets of books:  1) the private set of actual (real) incomes; and 2) the inflated revenues numbers they used to sell franchises. When we checked with the other franchisees, they also were duped and were struggling. The franchisees who purchased stores were too afraid of these guys to say anything to me when I talked to them during the due diligence period of pre-trial exploration. I later discovered the Franchisors were known to carry guns.

Finding out I had been duped by fraud, we began checking into the history of these guys selling franchises. They falsified their disclosures in their franchise documents. For example, they did not disclose their previous bankruptcy, which is illegal under franchise laws. Nor did they disclose regulation violations ... also illegal.

The franchising laws in this country are so detailed, thorough and inclusive that one can expect to be able to rely on disclosure documents as inclusive of all history of the Franchisors, both personal and business. I lost hundreds of thousands of dollars, not to mention the emotional wear and tear during the seven years it took to have my day in court. After seven years of trial preparation and research, I finally won my case for damages, plus the additional punitive damages awarded by the jury for fraud. However, in the end, I lost it all. I got nothing out of it. Vindictively, they had cancelled the insurance on the warehouse at signing it over. After years of fighting, I just did not have the time, energy or money to continue to try to overcome their fraudulent practices.

I do not know why this extraordinary chain of events happened to me. In reflection, I do not know what I would have done differently. I do wonder how people get through times like this without a strong faith in God. Sometimes, you simply must have a strong belief that He is in control, and He has you in the palm of His hand, regardless of what happens.

# $1,000 vs. $10,000

*"Give, and it shall be given unto you; good measure, pressed down, and shaken together, and running over, shall men give into your bosom. For with the same measure that ye mete withal it shall be measured to you again."* Luke 6:38

I was always asking God to allow me to be a mere conduit of funds to His Kingdom work. My life's verse is Luke 6:38.

My wife and I chose to support two missionaries in the Sudan in Africa. I went through at least a month of morning devotions where I felt God speaking to me and telling me to send the two missionaries a donation of $1,000. I mailed it to Florida, where they were home from the mission field in Africa on temporary furlough to do fundraising for their return trip.

About a week later, in my morning prayer time, I felt God say, "You missed a zero." I thought, "Surely it wasn't supposed to be $10,000?" I went into the kitchen and told my wife, Bertie, what I was feeling. I thought she would recoil when I mentioned the amount. Instead she said, "If you get this impression while in prayer, you must get the additional money up and send it to them." We discussed whether to send $9,000 additional to make it a total of $10,000 with the previous check, or if I were to send an additional $10,000. By now, they would have received the first $1,000. We both agreed that for some reason, it was important to make it total $10,000, so we sent another $9,000. In the note to them, we told them about the prompting of the Lord to send a total of $10,000, and that I felt earlier I had "missed it" by a zero when I sent only $1,000.

A week later, we got a call from them in Florida, telling us what an incredible donation ... both timing, and importance of the amount. It seems that they had a major donor, Mr. Anthony Rossi, founder of Tropicana, who gave their mission some large financial gifts. They were praying for more public, smaller gifts to satisfy their tax filings with the IRS for their non-profit. It seemed that they needed $10,000 more, but they also needed two additional donors. At their request, we agreed to let $5,000 be credited as a donation from Bertie, and $5,000 to come from me. This made up the two additional donors they needed, which solved their problem. They said they had been praying about the need for at least two more donors and an additional $10,000 every day, and that this was a direct answer to their prayers.

My obedience to that still, small voice of God in prayer was a direct answer to their prayers offered up at the same time. It is so great to know that you have been used by God to meet another's needs. The accurate promptings of God came from prayer and seeking Him. What a great feeling to know you are directly linked to God in prayer. He hears, answers, and speaks to us. We do not even need to know what other needs are, if we can only seek Him, and He can tell us what to do. Then, when we obey, others' needs and prayers are answered. How exciting! This interaction in prayer is an extraordinary event I wish everyone could experience.

# VISIONS

*"Your old men shall dream dreams, your young men
shall see visions." Joel 2:28*

I will have to confess that I am skeptical when people say they have had visions. I really do not know how to deal with that. However, having honestly said that, I feel compelled to tell you about an experience I had once, which felt like a vision to me.

Mid-day, I was sitting on the deck of my cabin in Atlanta while praying. It was peaceful, and I was lost in the sound of the river rapids just 20 feet or so from me. It was my idea of heaven. I had committed to tithing my time for a year. That is, I committed to Bible study and praying for the first 10% of my time each day. A 10% tithe of a day was 144 minutes, or 2-hours and 24 minutes. At the beginning of my day, I was spending that time in reading the Bible and praying, before I did anything else to start my days work. That day, I was making up time I had missed earlier that morning.

At this particular time, I was praying. I had been thinking about heaven, and what it would be like there. I had just read about God giving the "Crown of Righteousness", and I had been meditating on I Samuel 16, where the Lord told the prophet Samuel to anoint a son of Jesse to be King of Israel. After Jesse paraded his seven sons past Samuel, Samuel said to Jesse, "Are these all your children?" Then Jesse said that the youngest was out in the field tending the sheep. Samuel asked Jesse to bring the youngest son to him. When Samuel laid eyes on David, he said, "This is he," and he anointed David, King of Israel. When the father, Jesse, questioned why, the prophet Samuel said, "Man looks on the outward appearance, but God looks on the heart." That is why we need to make sure our *heart* is pure before God, regardless of what others see in us or think about us.

I was deep in thought, meditating on what heaven and its rewards would look like when we are judged on what God thought of us, compared to what man thought of us. Suddenly, with my eyes shut, the air got cool, and I was mentally transported to heaven. It was so peaceful, and I was behind the curtain of the stage in a huge auditorium and looking out on the audience filing in to take their seats. Somehow, I *knew* that God would hand out "awards" that night. Everyone was talking about who would win the "Crown of Righteousness." I could see the great TV evangelists elbowing for positions on the front rows and others meekly taking whatever seats were available, no matter how far back or up in the balcony. Although I could not place a face on anyone taking their seats, I somehow *knew* the various TV and major church personalities positioning to be up front, much as they had done on earth. I am glad they were actually faceless. I strangely *knew* who they were here on earth, although I cannot explain how I *knew* that without being able to *see* their faces.

A hush fell over the auditorium when God stepped to the podium. As the front row of famous ministers edged up to the front of their seats, God announced the name of the saint who would be the recipient of the "Crown of Righteousness." When He said the name, it was a woman that evidently no one knew. Everyone in the auditorium was asking those to either side of them if they knew who the lady was. Finally, after coaxing, an old lady in the furthest row in the back of the upper balcony stood up. She began making her way sheepishly over to the aisle, and down the aisle to begin the long walk down the steps to the lower auditorium level. I was aware of the extreme level of disappointment in the crowd, as well as the mystery of who this person was that she would be receiving the "Crown of Righteousness." No one seemed to know her. As she was coming, God quietly reminded the crowd that HE judged on the heart, not outward appearance, accomplishments or earthly acclaim.

At that point, I "woke up" from my "trance" and vision, and became aware of my surroundings. While I wondered why I was shown this scene, I suddenly thought of my mother. Now, I do not think, nor can I say, that the woman receiving the "Crown of Righteousness" was actually my mother. However, it was a situation *like* that of my mother. When she passed away and we went into her house, sitting beside my father's recliner were two shoeboxes of note cards with people's names on them. They sat on upside-down, plastic crates to give easier height access to the notes. They were notes of prayer requests and included the dates that mother had prayed for those people's prayer requests.

There were articles and newspaper clippings about people injured in accidents attached to the back of the note card, with the dates that mother had prayed for them. There were addresses of prisoners with receipts clipped to the back of the note card indicating that mother had ordered a leather Bible with the prisoners name stamped in gold on the front, with the date she had shipped it to them in prison, along with their prayer request that she prayed for them.

There was a note about when she heard a pastor speak about an urgent need for $300, and she put $300 cash in an envelope addressed in red ink. She had my sister drive to another town to mail the gift, so it would not have a Tulsa postmark on it and they would not know the source of the gift. There was another note about when she heard a testimony of the miraculous receipt of the $300 in an envelope *addressed in red ink without a return address* on it. This was my mother's confirmation that the pastor received her cash that God told her to send to him.

There was an article about the Tulsa John 3:16 Rescue Mission for the homeless closing their doors for lack of funds. With it, there was a note about how my mother had my sister take cash to the Mission anonymously to keep its doors open. It is still ministering to homeless people today in downtown Tulsa.

I just know this ... God looks on the heart. I think when we get to heaven, there will be those who receive reward for their extraordinary heart and heart actions, that none of us here on earth know about. It will be easy to see what the notable, famous workers in the Kingdom have done. But, I think we will be surprised at the heavenly mansions given to those we esteemed least here on earth, because we judged on the outward appearances of fame, visible accomplishments, and advertised work done for the Kingdom. God judges on the heart, humility, meekness, purity of motives, and the relationship with the Lord. Those that are least here on earth just may be first in the Kingdom. After all, Matthew 19:30 says: *"But many that are first shall be last; and the last shall be first."*

# LIVING THROUGH 9/11

*"For He shall give his angels charge over thee,*
*to keep thee in all thy ways."* Psalms 91:11

They say that no one ever forgets where they were when they became aware of the events that occurred at 8:45 AM on September 11, 2001, when the planes hit the World Trade Center towers. I was in the home office of StarTouch International in the suburbs of Atlanta. StarTouch was the parent company that owned Promise-Net International, the telecommunications company where I was President. I saw everyone grouped around a TV set with exclamations of, "Oh No," and "Oh my God. This can't be happening." I went over to the group of huddled employees and saw the news video footage of planes flown into the World Trade Center towers.

"Oh my God," I thought. "My oldest daughter, Catherine, works in Tower II." I immediately dialed her cell, but no response. It appeared dead. I was so worried. It was the beginning of the workday, so she would normally be there. In a panic at the time, it did not occur to me that twin towers were the tallest buildings in New York City, and most of the cell phone towers were on top of them. The knot in the pit of my stomach became stronger, knowing my daughter might be trapped in Tower II as I watched the towers burn. I began alternately dialing her cell and office number to no avail. My attempts to call her alternated with prayers for God to save her somehow.

I spent hours and hours in pure agony, while listening for some news of survivors. I was hoping to hear anything to give a spark of hope. I had left voice mail messages on her cell, but if the towers were down, no cell phone signals were being transmitted. At a time like that, your thoughts jump around from, "What an incredible, unique person she is." "We invested so much to get her to this point." "It would be such a waste if we lost her … If the world lost her …" "I love her so much."

Finally, 3 ½ hours later, there was a call. "I'm OK," Catherine said. "I didn't go in to New York today." She was in her condominium, the Galaxy, three round 50-story towers on the water's edge of the New Jersey shore overlooking Manhattan. She actually saw the plane hit Tower II where she worked. Scheduled for a business trip to the Netherlands, she needed to update her passport. She decided that the lines would be shorter in Hackensack, New Jersey, than in New York. Therefore, she headed up the New Jersey coast that morning. That choice, along with the province of God, probably saved her life.

Amazingly enough, no one in her office perished. The office manager, having lived through the Twin Towers parking garage bombings years ago, recognized the explosion sounds and shutters of the building. He ordered everyone to follow him to the ground floor, took the subway ten stops away and surfaced to place a call to headquarters. That is when he found out from the newscasts that planes were purposely flown into the Towers to destroy them. His quick action had saved the lives of all those working in his office on the 26th floor of Tower II. Many people perished that day, and there are many extraordinary stories of people whose lives were saved. I am so grateful to God that my daughter was one of those whose life was saved. I had often prayed Psalms 91 over my household and my daughters.

# PROPHECIES

*"Remember ye not the former things, neither consider the things of old. Behold, I will do a new thing; now it shall spring forth; shall ye not know it? I will even make a way in the wilderness, and rivers in the desert."* Isaiah 43:18-19

I was in Dallas, Texas, at a meeting of the Christian Oilmen's Association. Suddenly, the speaker to the assembly, Dick Mills, stopped and said; "I have a word from God for that man back there," pointing in my direction. I was 30-40 rows from the front. It was not easy to see with whom he was trying to make eye contact. Still pointing in my direction, he began to call out, "The man with glasses … in the red sweater." I raised off my seat a little, saying, "Me?"

He nodded and said, "Yes, please stand up." He said, "The Lord told me to give the verses Isaiah 43:18 and 19 for your life. He is going to do a new thing, and you should not consider the things of old." I sat down, and he went right on speaking, as if there had been no interruption at all. I did not know what to make of this. The meeting completed, and I was still in wonder at being singled out like that in a large public meeting. It felt so powerful and so unusual that I wrote the date and speaker's name in the margin of my Bible next to Isaiah 43:18-19. "WOW! I am making a half-million per year income. This must mean I am going to get rich. It is going to be great … this 'new thing!' I can't imagine it getting better than this," I thought.

Less than a year later, I was in Nashville, Tennessee, at another meeting. Once again, a different speaker stopped in the middle of his speech, singled me out of the audience and asked me to stand. He said, "I feel impressed by the Lord to tell you that He is going to do a new thing in your life, and that you should not consider the former things." He also referenced Isaiah 43:18-19. I sat down, and he continued with his talk. WOW... two times now, from two different speakers, in two different states.

Being called out of a crowd and given the same verses happened twice more subsequently, with two different speakers, in two different meetings in different towns. It was overwhelming! I did not know what to do with that information. I could only assume that I was in for a "new thing" in my life somewhere down the road, and I surmised I was not to be surprised by it, but to cling to the prophecies and know the changes were ordained as from the Lord. I was a little excited, yet a little concerned. Is it going to be a big thing? Why would God move to have men tell me this so many times? Is the 'new thing' going to be good ... or bad?

Soon after these call-outs, the Tax Reform Act of 1986 passed Congress, and President Reagan signed it into law. Real estate values quickly began to crumble. The investors were losing their tax write-offs, stopped making their contributions, and allowing the foreclosures of their units. I suddenly began to have claims against me as the General Partner of all my limited partnerships. My business began to spiral downward. As General Partner, I only had 5-10% ownership of the syndicated apartment projects, but I had 100% of the liability for the mortgages and the debts. When the limited partners stopped making their payments, the lenders came after me, the General Partner. It took a decade and a half to unwind all those partnerships and properties. In addition, it was not just me. A subsidiary of American Express had 300 apartment projects in foreclosure. The Act even took the Savings and Loan industry down and broke them all. After 14 years of hell, I was free of all business entanglements. The bank foreclosed on my 11,000 square foot home, and my wife of 32 years died of cancer. I lost three businesses. You could say that this was a "new thing." I just did not know the "new thing" was going to be so bad. On the other hand, was the "new thing" going to be good because everything was now so bad?

Being free of all entanglements, I was finally able to accept Larry Burkett's request to work for him. Larry was the founder of Christian Financial Concepts, Inc., which taught biblical principles of handling money. He had repeatedly asked me to work with him. I was his original Board Member, but I was making too much money to quit and go into ministry. This resolved itself by events beyond my control ... the "new thing."

I accepted the position of acting President for CFC. There, I was able to witness the life-changes the ministry made in people's lives as they implemented Larry's teachings of biblical principles for handling money in their lives.

After Larry passed away from cancer, CFC merged into CROWN Ministries and I left CFC. I was free to accept the position of Executive Director of Faith Farm Ministries, a free 9-month drug and alcohol addiction recovery ministry, with 445 beds located on 1,500 acres in three cities of South Florida. This is the best job ever! I get to witness dramatic changes in peoples' lives on a daily basis. It truly is a 'new thing' and nothing like the things of old.

I never would have dreamed of such a change in direction for my life, although I was warned ... many times. I could never have conceived of a job with so much satisfaction ... the satisfaction of seeing your life's work resulting in the dramatic turnaround of lives from drugs and alcohol into transformed new creations in Christ.

This is definitely a "new thing" and an extraordinary experience. It is an honor to be a part of it.

# eHARMONY.com

*"And the Lord God said, it is not good that
the man should be alone."* Genesis 2:18

Without a wife, I felt so alone. I was "plumbed and wired" to be married. After my wife of over 32 years died of cancer, I needed companionship.

One Sunday afternoon while in my home office, I was on my computer during the NASCAR race, which was on the TV behind me. I heard an advertisement come on for eHarmony.com, and I swiveled around in my chair to watch it. They claimed they put a lot of care into providing "matches" based upon characteristics, personality, beliefs, values, core traits, personal preferences and compatibility. They got my attention. It sure sounded like a great "shortcut" to screening preferences, compared to multiple dates with multiple people, and wasted time, energy and expense of initial dating. I was into efficiency. The only thing ... they required a thorough profile be filled out online, which the ad said could be done in a couple of hours or less. That was how they "jump-started" the search game to provide the better matches. *"It sounded reasonable,"* I thought. Therefore, I went to their web site, signed up, and began answering questions to start building my profile of likes and dislikes. Upon completion, I awaited for the first match to my profile, preferences and age group.

Because my deceased wife and I had been separated by almost 930 miles when we met (Tulsa, Oklahoma, to Greenville, South Carolina), I was not spooked by distance. I put no mileage limitations on my eHarmony profile. Little did I realize that I would eventually get over a thousand matches in just one year, from Florida to Alaska? That was impossible to manage. The communication with matches required a lot of asking questions of each match and answering questions from each match, all designed to get a deeper knowledge of each match. Moreover, that was all by typing. I never typed so much in my life! *"If only I could retake my final timed college typing test now,"* I thought.

The typing process did serve to shed light on things quickly, though. For example, several women "dropped me" from communication because they were in "Alabama" and I was in the adjacent state of Georgia. "Too far away to date," they said. Well, that told me a lot ... just how small their world was as compared to mine. I had traveled to 50 countries, and my first wife of 32 years of marriage was at school in Greenville, South Carolina, when I met her. I was 930 miles away in Tulsa, Oklahoma. We met, dated, married, and lived happily for over 32 years, starting from that far away. Comments and "drops" like that were great, fast "screens" for this process, even though our profiles, backgrounds, and preferences created the match. Other telling signs, like fear of distance, said volumes to me about how big (or small) their world was. I do not deny they were practical in their assessment, but not as venturesome as I am. Just the communication overload alone was overwhelming. I went into my personal profile settings and dropped the mileage limitations for matches from "no limits" to "300 miles" (from Atlanta). Fortunately, the change did not happen until after I received a match from Chicago, Illinois ... the match I married.

Before I traveled to meet my Chicago match, "Cindy," I had some dates with matches in Atlanta. The sudden drop in matches due to my geographical limitations allowed me to narrow my communication to more local matches, better questions and answers to their questions, and scheduling of actual dates. I was also able to avoid the more blatant and obviously overt suggestive comments and photos from "Vanessa," "Georgia," and "Bambi." The eHarmony.com founder, Dr. Neil Clark Warren, had set up strict rules for the first meeting: 1) lunch; 2) daylight; 3) public place; and 4) a string of friends to call you every 30 minutes so that you could report that you were "OK" ... *"All good, safe rules to go by,"* I thought.

No matter who I matched, went out with, or talked to, I kept coming back to one of my earliest matches before I limited the mileage away from me; Cynthia A. Miller (Cindy) in Chicago. She actually lived in the more romantically named suburb of Romeoville, Illinois. Imagine ... finding a princess in "Romeoville." I seemed to "click" with her and wanted to see a picture of her. After all, I had posted my photo up front when I filled out my profile. I felt she should have done the same. However, Cindy had trouble getting her picture posted on-line. Her excuses sounded plausible, but I finally reached a point where I simply was not going to move toward her any more without seeing a picture of her. I had a good reason.

I connected with a very pleasant woman in Alabama, until I demanded she post her picture on line, and she did. I quit. As sweet as she was, I just could not see myself waking up every morning to someone who looked like she had been a model for the artist who drew the University of Georgia Bulldog caricature. I know that sounds harsh, but life is real. Another lady I met obviously could not find a more "recent" photo to post than one taken at least 15 years earlier. Get real. Why are we playing games here? Whom do we think we will eventually fool? We were wasting time. Therefore, I pushed Cindy to post a recent photo. With technical help, she finally got it to work and posted her photo.

275

After months of typing communications, I finally saw a photo of her.

WOW! I was looking at a short, cute blonde-haired woman who looked nowhere near her posted age. I thought, "How could she get to be that age and be that cute, and never been married?" She was extraordinary! I had to meet her in person. I made plans to travel to Chicago to meet one of my earliest matches, and take her to dinner. This appeared to be just too good to be true. (Read all about it in the chapter, "Meeting Cindy.")

# MEETING CINDY

*"Whoso findeth a wife findeth a good thing,*
*and obtaineth favour of the Lord."* Proverbs 18:22

I finally arranged to meet my eHarmony.com match in Chicago. As I was getting off the plane in Chicago's O'Hare International Airport, I shook off the thought, *"if something happened to me, no one knows I'm here ... no friends ... not my children, no one."* I could never tell my kids that I was internet dating. I was just too *respectable* for that.

I called Cindy's cell to tell her I had landed, and she informed me that she was stuck in traffic on the Interstate and could be up to an hour late. I said I would wait in the Delta arrival section in the last area of the median furthest from the baggage claim doors.

I was standing and leaning against the wall watching a very energetic short, young Hispanic man in a bright yellow traffic vest with a whistle in his mouth. He was waving his arms and keeping the traffic moving, while one-by-one drivers negotiated their auto over to the curb to pick up their arriving loved ones, load the bags into the trunk and then pull away from the curb. This young man used his whistle and arms to help them negotiate their reentry from the curb into the bumper-to-bumper traffic feeding into the masses trying to exit the terminal area.

Plane after planeload of passengers waiting beside me found their ride, while I still waited. Finally, when I guess his curiosity could stand it no more, he came over to me during a brief lull in traffic, and asked, "Senõr, are you waiting for your wife?" I replied, "No." Evidently, his curiosity would not let him rest. After helping more cars pick up their passengers at the curb and reenter the traffic flow, he came over to me again and asked, "Then, who are you waiting for?" I finally told him, "Someone I met on the internet."

"Do you know what she looks like?" he asked. "Sure," I said, opening my briefcase and showing him her picture.

"How do you know that's her … If that is really her picture?"

A little bit of fear crept in at that point, but I countered with "Well, she should look like this," I said.

"What is she driving?" he asked. I told him, "She has two red Volkswagens; a convertible for sunny days and a hardtop named 'Gretta the Jetta'." Since it was a little rainy out, I told him to look out for the red hardtop. He began the lookout for a red VW Jetta sandwiched in traffic.

"Senõr," he asked. "Does anyone know you're here?" Again, a wall of worry crept into my mind. I asked him, "Why are you asking these questions?"

He said, "Because, Senõr, on the news last month, a man came to Chicago to meet someone he connected with over the internet and was killed by a transvestite. How can you be sure that she actually sent you a picture of her and not someone else?"

"Oh … my … God," I thought. I did not want anyone to know I was internet dating. I did not want anyone to know I was sneaking off to Chicago on Friday night for a dinner date to meet someone.

I do not have blood pressure problems, but when he said that, I felt flush … like I was going to faint. I led a moral life. I have always done the right thing. I have always been good. Now, suddenly, I may be found dead in an alley (if I were to be found) with the police trying to match dental records on my corpse. What would my family think? I was trying to leave a Godly legacy. Would my family buy this one? Was this to be the final memory of me? I have often said, "It's not how you start, but how you finish that folks will remember." Is this it? This is how I will be remembered … sneaking off to Chicago to meet someone I met on the Internet?

Suddenly, his arms waiving and whistle blowing, he directs a red Jetta to the curb in front of me. Through the windshield, it looked "like" Cindy's picture. When she got out of her car on the driver's side, stood up, and I spotted that cute blonde hair on her, I was relieved. Actually, I was more than that. I was "smitten." Her smile was so happy. Nevertheless, I could not miss the sight of the traffic cop standing in the middle of the center lane behind her, looking her up and down, while he gave a "thumbs up" with both hands and smiling approvingly. He was jumping up and down, as if he was on a springy pogo stick with both thumbs in the air. All was well. Fear gone and scary stories forgotten, we met in person for the first time and embraced.

After loading my suitcase and getting in on the passenger side for her to drive us to our dinner reservation, I noticed a long list of names and phone numbers taped to the dash. Being conditioned to Dr. Warren's *rules*, I spent the next hour on the interstate calling everyone on the list: a sister in Houston; a mother in Coal City; a retired Nun in Joliett; and others who might be concerned about whom Cindy was meeting. (I *knew* I was nice … I never thought that her family and friends might be worried.) Actually, as a woman, she was taking a greater risk than I was. While Cindy drove, I talked with everyone on her list to put their minds at ease that I was actually nice and not some serial killer, who made connections with his victims on the internet.

Cindy said she was 38.9 in mental and energy years. She admitted to being a little older in earth years. She looked so good. For a moment, I was worried that I was "robbing the cradle" until I remembered that we all had filled out profiles, and eHarmony.com had certain age limitation spreads for their matches. I knew she could not possibly be 38 no matter how great she looked because of the eHarmony.com maximum age spread allowance. I felt safe that I was not "robbing the cradle." It sure looked like I was … she was cute. As I said earlier, I was "smitten." This was extraordinarily unusual in the grand scheme of life events.

Meet Cindy

Cindy's first visit to my cabin on the Yellow River in the Stone Mountain Park area of Atlanta. Cindy had a framed picture of a cabin in her home because she had always wanted to live in a log cabin.

# FED BY THE BROOK

*"And it shall be, that thou shalt drink of the brook; and I have commanded the ravens to feed thee there."* I Kings 17:4

The decline of the real estate market caused my termination as Director of Acquisitions for a real estate firm in Atlanta on February 2, 2006. Their reasoning for the termination and shutdown of the entire acquisition department was if their existing projects were not profitable (and they were not, having been added to their portfolio long before I got there), why would they add more? This sounded logical to me, except it was my head on the block.

The company decided to shut down the Acquisitions Department. It happened suddenly and without notice when I came in to work one morning. It caught me totally by surprise, especially since the week before; I had expressed my concern about lack of profitability of previously acquired projects to the President. She told me, "Your concerns are unfounded – you have nothing to worry about." While they say, "knowledge is power," this looked more like ignorance is bliss to me. They finally woke up and acknowledged the problem. However, it appeared to me they shot the messenger.

I always had people knocking on my door to offer me more money or a higher position. I never lost a job in my whole life. This really caught me off guard. Since leaving the Navy for the Merrill Lynch position, I never had to do a job search.

I went on unemployment and did job searches on-line. I created a Resume' and sent it to dozens of companies, non-profits, posted it on-line and networked with every group I could find in

Atlanta. I soon found out that the most difficult time to get a job is when you do not currently have one.

I had no savings or reserves, and the unemployment ran out in six months. At that time, there were no extensions. I added financial needs to my prayer list, along with needing a job. Fortunately, the 140-year-old cabin I lived in by the Yellow River was debt-free, so I had no mortgage. (Thank you, Larry Burkett, for your teachings.) Even then, I could not pay my bills for utilities, taxes, insurance, food, etc. I took early Social Security before age 65. I received much less monthly income than if I waited to full retirement age, but I was so desperate for money. I continued to pray every day. I still needed money for taxes, insurance, food, gas, dry cleaning, laundry, etc. – I needed to keep up appearances while networking and trying to get interviews.

One day, when I was quickly becoming destitute, there was a knock on the cabin door. An attorney I used when I went into business for myself after leaving Merrill Lynch came to my home. I had not seen him in over a decade. He slowly told me he could not speak well because of a recent stroke. He handed me a piece of paper on which he had written a note that said, "I know you probably don't need this, but God has spoken to me and told me to give this to you." When I looked up from reading his note, he reached into his shirt pocket and pulled out a folded check. When I opened it, I was shocked to see it was for $5,000.

WOW! While I was in prayer for funds, God was then speaking to him to give me those funds. I learned that when you are praying for money, you have to be patient and trust Him. God is not a counterfeiter who will rain money down from heaven. You must wait for Him not only speak to someone about what you are praying for, but they must be willing to listen to Him as well. In addition, they must obey Him, and do it. It takes all of it ... work, prayer, listening, obedience, action ... ALL of it, together. I had often been the answer to other's prayers. This time, it reversed. It was happening to me ... to meet my needs.

I had always been a "giver," but now, I needed to be the recipient. I have found that true prosperity is not being wealthy with money stored up. You can lose it all with one bad move. In fact, wealth is a vapor. Wealth can be wiped out by the stroke of a pen. After I lost my millions due to the Tax Reform Act of 1986, I found out that laws and other events could change your life and make your wealth a vapor. In fact, I once opened a public speaking engagement with one of my credentials as having a "doctorate in vapors." I have had the pleasure of giving to others to meet their needs, and in my time of need, someone now gave to me. Sometimes, God uses you to meet the needs of others. Sometimes you have needs for others to meet. This is actually the way it is supposed to work in God's economy. Nevertheless, it was extraordinary having someone respond to God that I had not seen or spoken to in over 10 years. God speaking to them from my cries and prayers for financial help, to seek me out and give me $5,000 to sustain me until I could get a job ... I believe this was nothing short of incredible! No logical mind could deny that this interaction in the Spiritual realm is extraordinary.

# HEADHUNTER PURSUIT

*"Seest thou a man diligent in his business? He shall stand before kings." Proverbs 22:29*

"Stop bothering me," I thought. "I don't want to move to South Florida in the heat and humidity. I have been happy in Atlanta for 35 years. My two daughters, their husbands, four grandsons, a granddaughter, and the home I love on the river are all here. Why should I move away for that job?" After all, her job search for Faith Farm Ministries was relentless. She was certain I was perfect for the job, but I did not want to travel to Florida to interview. "Would I at least interview on the phone?" she said. "OK, I could agree to do that," I told her.

They set up a time for me to receive a call from three Board Members of Faith Farm. When they called, they made it clear that there were other candidates, and they wanted to treat each candidate fairly. They informed me that they decided each call to a candidate was to be limited to exactly one hour. They would ask a series of 15 questions, and I would have 3 minutes to respond to each question. The final 15 minutes of the hour phone interview was open for follow-up questions, or for me to ask my questions, if any. We began.

They asked me about spiritual opinions, retail experience, management experience, hard decisions I would be required to make, my opinions on various business pursuits, advertising experience, feelings about caring for the indigent population, and just about every other thing concerning business management. I noticed that our time was far exceeding the hour they allotted, and I had not yet asked my questions. I did not say anything about exceeding their self-imposed time limits. The follow-up questions were coming from all three Board members and I was answering them quickly and thoroughly. Suddenly, the Board Treasurer said, "We've been unfair. We are well past two hours on this call, so this is unfair to the other candidates. We've given too much time to Mr. Webb's call." Trying to end the phone call, they all were concerned. They had more questions. I had answered all their questions well, and they wanted to know more. Instead of asking more questions, they allowed more time for me to ask the questions that I had, after which they said their goodbyes and told me I would hear from the Talent Search representative later.

I was intrigued but not fully sold on the organization. After all, it was still in South Florida. Even though I had been CEO of several other organizations, this was a drug and alcohol recovery ministry. I had no experience with addiction; much less know how to minister to addicts. Later, I began receiving calls from the headhunter. After hearing the Board search committee's response to my phone interview, she wanted me to go to Florida and look at the organization. She still believed I was perfect for the job of Executive Director. I continued to disregard her insistence. I just did not want to move away from Atlanta. When released from active duty in the Navy, I had purposely selected to move to Atlanta. After visiting 12 cities in the South as possible hometowns, Atlanta won. I moved there 35 years earlier. I was happy with my decision, and my children and grandchildren were there.

I attended an investment seminar in Orlando with my brother, Jerry, because he was a top producer in financial planning with a certain organization, and they paid the way for the top producers to attend conventions in top resorts. He was always honored with awards. They also allowed full expenses for a guest, and he asked me to join him there as his guest, at their expense. Since I was broke, this was a real vacation treat.

We were laying by the pool on Saturday, our last day in Orlando before flying out on Sunday. I received another call on my cell from the headhunter. I had been dodging her calls for days. I answered my cell this time, because I could not see the screen in the bright sunlight while sitting by the pool,

I recognized Ginger's voice. "Where are you?" she asked. "In Orlando" I replied. "Oh Great," she said. "You are less than a half days drive to Faith Farm." "Please go see it," she asked.

It seemed convenient to make a flight change back to Atlanta, rent a car, and drive down. So I agreed. Moreover, I would finally get her off my back. Instead of flying back to Atlanta on Sunday, I would rent a car and drive from Orlando to Ft. Lauderdale, Florida. I requested Faith Farm to arrange for a car and driver to pick me up early Monday morning and take me to each of the three Farms in one day. I could see them all and then decide if I wanted to interview with the Board of Directors on Tuesday, the following evening. On Sunday, I headed down to Fort Lauderdale. They accommodated me in a guest apartment Sunday night. At 6:00 AM the next morning, the Interim Executive Director, Mike Guthrie, picked me up, and we headed out to visit all three farms in Okeechobee, Boynton Beach in Palm Beach County, and then back to Ft. Lauderdale, the original Faith Farm location. Mike patiently took all day and showed me the entire operation, driving me to all three Farms.

By the third farm location, I was smitten and my heart was touched by the interaction of the men in the Program with the loving staff members. This made me want consideration for the top

289

position of Executive Director. I agreed to attend the Board meeting the following evening to continue the interview. Every question asked by a Board Member exposed an area of my expertise from previous business experiences that prepared me for this job.

I received no indication of their response to my interview. I went back to their apartment, slept, and drove to Orlando the next morning to catch my return flight to Atlanta. After a week or so, I drove to my brother's Arkansas retreat away from his Chicago investment-planning firm for a visit. While there, I received an email offer of employment from Faith Farm. The Board President gave me his number to call him. He said he needed to speak with me concerning one of my conditions of receiving an offer from them. I told him I needed it to be a unanimous vote by the Board to bring me on. I told him that I could deal with any problem under my authority, but I could not deal with dissention or disagreement between those above me to whom I answered … in this case, the Board of Directors. Therefore, it had to be a unanimous vote for me to come as a condition of my accepting any offer.

When I called him, he wanted to talk to me about my unanimous vote conditional requirement. He said there were two older men that voted "No." However, when questioned why they would vote "No," one of the men said he simply did not understand some things. When explained to him, he changed his vote to "Yes." At that same time, he also said he felt he was probably too old to serve on the Board, and he resigned. The second Board member that voted no had a heart attack on the way home and had to resign. The Board President said, "Based upon those circumstances, I consider that a unanimous vote. How do you see it?" It seemed clear to me that God wanted me to be there, since He eradicated the sources of the "No" votes. Therefore, I said "Yes" and accepted their offer to come as Executive Director of Faith Farm Ministries.

Looking back, I do not know why I was so resistant. Humidity … Heat … What is important? I almost missed it. Faith Farm is the greatest ministry I ever encountered. We take drug and alcohol addicts off the street, clean them up, house, feed, clothe, and train them for 9 months, then put them back on the street as productive citizens. By the time they've completed 9 months, they have obtained their GED, resolved all their records (Social Security, birth certificate, drivers license, library card), had an opportunity to test for college credits in the courses they are obligated to take in the Program, plus receive a job opportunity or a scholarship to school, depending upon their interests and desires. We try to eliminate any excuse they might have for not being successful. I love it. It is the greatest job I have ever had, because I get to witness a total transformation of lives. I experience incredible job satisfaction … seeing the greatest life changes I have ever personally witnessed. Each graduation speech is an extraordinary witness of a dramatically changed life. Talk about job satisfaction! Moreover, I almost missed it!

# A FOUR LETTER WORD

*"And put a knife to thy throat, if thou be a man given to appetite."* Proverbs 23:2

At the insistence of a Headhunter in Atlanta, I traveled to South Florida and interviewed with the Board of Directors of a drug and alcohol recovery ministry, who hired that search firm to find an Executive Director. I did not want to go to South Florida because I do not like heat and humidity. However, my heart melted when I visited the ministry. I took the offered position of Executive Director of Faith Farm Ministries.

As with many of my other previous rookie CEO positions, I did not have any experience with drugs, alcohol, or recovery. A sampling of other industries where I had no experience but was employed as the CEO was a telecommunications company, investment syndications, apartment acquisition and rehabilitation, a financial non-profit and others. In each case, as quickly as possible, I jumped right into the job and learned as much as possible about what I was to "manage."

When I went to South Florida in June 2007, Faith Farm Ministries was a 56-year-old ministry providing a free, 9-month, residential drug and alcohol residential recovery program for men and women. An estimated 30,000 people had come through the program during the 56 years and had their lives changed. Faith Farm provides the student with a bed, clothes, food, classes, chapel services and a work-training program. They are given classroom instruction on the causes of addiction, how to rebuild the walls of their lives, how to set boundaries for when they leave and re-encounter their past old influences, understanding the grace of God, and especially spiritual counseling and training. Students are

293

cocooned in a loving environment for nine months until graduation. If they do not have a high school diploma, they have a chance to earn a GED. In their final class, they are given help in creating a Resume', job search skills, help with a scholarship if they want to go to school, and help with getting non-convicted arrests expunged from their records. In short, Faith Farm makes every effort to override any excuse for not being successful. Students receive a "jump start" to a new life. In addition, they have the opportunity to take exams and earn up to nine (9) free college credits from an accredited college for courses taken over the nine months in the Program.

The three campuses are located on a total of 1,500 acres. The three South Florida locations are Ft. Lauderdale (13 acres), Boynton Beach (90 acres), and Okeechobee (1,400 acres). Graduations occur every 6 weeks at each Farm, and I travel to each campus to a graduation three out of every six Sundays. I hear many different graduation speeches by graduates sharing something about their past, circumstances that brought them to Faith Farm and the changes God has made in their lives while in the Program. At the beginning, I had difficulty relating to their stories of out-of-control drinking and drug usage.

I come from a very conservative background. My father was a minister, and a very strict one at that. No movies, no dancing, and no cards or dice were allowed in our home. No smoking, no drinking, and certainly no mixed bathing, i.e., swimming with girls in swimsuits (and that was back when they were all one-piece swimsuits). I was sheltered growing up, and I never encountered anyone who drank or did drugs. In fact, I somehow got the impression that anyone who participated in those activities was simply an undisciplined, "low life." Because I was never put in a tragic position of having low self esteem due to parental verbal badgering, an abusive situation, or any other thing that would "drive a person to drink" (as some would say), I was having difficulty relating to these men and women. I did not understand the reasons why they believed drinking was a way to forget, or drugs seemed pleasurable as a way to escape. I so desperately wanted to understand where they were coming from, other than my incorrect, narrow opinion that they were simply undisciplined individuals that just needed to get over it. I did not feel that I could ever be empowered with the empathy I needed to minister to them. I kept trying to figure out how to get there, but I simply could not get there on my own.

One Sunday morning after church, I came home to my apartment over my office, loosened my necktie, fell back across my bed in frustration and said, "God, I am not leaving here until You speak to me and tell me how I can understand someone who does something so uncontrollable in drinking or drugs. Why do they simply try, but can't have the will power to just stop ... just simply to quit." After all, I reasoned, I had quit smoking years ago. I just decided to stop one day, crumbled up the pack of cigarettes in my hand, tossed them in the trashcan, and quit. No withdrawals ... no problem ... I just decided to quit, and I did.

Well, I laid there for over an hour. This was very hard for me to do because the NASCAR race had already started, and my favorite driver, Jeff Gordon, was starting first on the pole. I was looking forward to seeing the race, and I had already missed the excitement of the green flag to start the race. Lying there was excruciating. Two hours ... Three hours ... I said, "God, I am NOT getting up from here until You speak to me. I need to understand why someone can be so out of control that they would let drugs or alcohol take over control their lives and then not have the power to just stop." They know not to use, but use anyway!

After almost four hours, I heard God speak in my spirit ... NOT audibly, but in that still, small voice inside that was so LOUD, it might as well have been an audible scream. The sound I heard inside my spirit was the word, "FOOD".

Suddenly, I understood it all. I broke down in tears and sobbed. The epiphany of understanding was overwhelming; comprehending someone being determined not to do something, yet doing it repeatedly ... That is me! I was always in a battle with my weight. I always was trying a new diet, a new fad, a new diet book, a new plan ... anything to be able to control my eating. I love to eat, and portion control was difficult for me. The result was that I was always fighting my waistline. I vowed not to eat ice cream at night, but could not control myself enough not to indulge. I always wanted just one more helping. I knew better, but I did it anyway ... FOOD ... that four-letter word brought full understanding of compulsive activity. Suddenly, I could relate to one who just could not stop doing something they knew they should not do. They knew it was bad, but they continued to do it anyway. I did not abuse nicotine, alcohol or drugs, but I now understand how that can happen (repeatedly) because I battle with eating urges beyond my basic needs. Moreover, as a result, I can understand and now have empathy to minister to those who have that addiction problem. Mine is the same compulsiveness, just a different product.

I should remember that Proverbs 23:2 does say, *"And put a knife to thy throat, if thou be a man given to appetite."* God was so good to speak to me in my arena of challenge so I would understand why people are compelled to do what they know they should not do, and do it repeatedly. I was the same as them, only with a different "addiction." What an extraordinary revelation. Thank You, God.

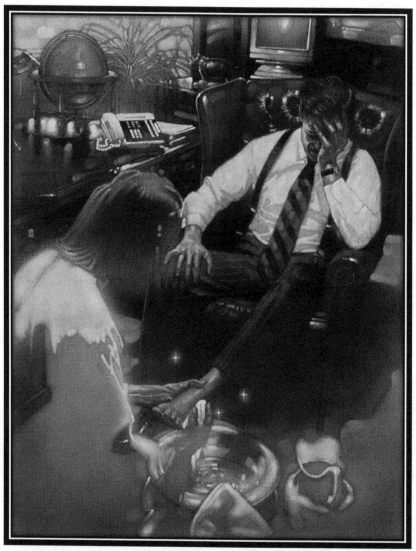

This picture entitled "The Servant" is on my wall above my office chair lest I forget my role as CEO

# A GIRL NAMED SUE

*"For the Lord shall be thy confidence."* Proverbs 3:26

I was sweating it! Would the Board of Directors feel like I was "playing" with them? What would they think? How was this going to turn out? I just had to know that I could trust them.

I moved to Palm Beach County, Florida, to take the Executive Director's position of a 56-year-old nonprofit organization. With over 90 staff members and employees, we needed a Director of Human Resources (HR). We needed a Director of HR to write policies and handle employee relations, benefits and the retirement plan. The search firm finally proposed a top candidate for the Board to interview in person. This HR professional was with a firm that had 2,600 employees and was really over qualified for our small nonprofit firm. However, she wanted to move to Florida and was willing to move, even though we were a much smaller, Christian nonprofit organization. We were flying this top candidate from Pennsylvania for an interview by the Board at the Tuesday evening's Board meeting.

The Monday morning prior to the Tuesday Board meeting, the search firm recruiter from Atlanta called me. She said, "I might be shooting myself in the foot, but I have another candidate named Sue that I feel might also be a perfect fit for you. Since she is in the local area, we could have her come to your office. If you like her, you can then decide whether to include her for an interview tomorrow night."

As the recruiter suggested, we called and met with Sue. We were very happy with her. Confirming that she was in the local area, we asked her to come to the Board meeting the following night for an interview. We told her she was one of two candidates interviewing with the Board that night. Both women showed up.

After interviewing both women, the Board of Directors could not decide which one should receive the employment offer. The candidate we flew in from Philadelphia had experience with 2,600 employees and was very qualified … almost too qualified for our smaller organization of less than 90 employees. Meanwhile, Sue, the local candidate, was an HR administrator over much smaller staffs, yet had more varied experience, including Doctors, Hospitals, Contractors, etc. After much discussion, the Board could not come to a consensus. The Board decided to pray and call in their votes to the Board Secretary by noon on Thursday. After praying, the Board Chair said the majority of votes called in for each individual would determine whom we hired.

Meanwhile, the next morning, the candidate from Philadelphia came to my office and said she was withdrawing her name from consideration because she did not think she would fit into this religious culture. When I told the Board Secretary of our conversation, she said, "Great! I'll call the Board and tell them that Sue will be the one."

I said, "No! Let the votes play out." As the new Executive Director, I needed to know that I was able to trust the Board when they say they will pray about the choice, and I needed to know that they were hearing from God.

We waited while each of the Board Members called in their votes, without telling any of them that the candidate from Philadelphia had asked me to withdraw her from consideration. Miraculously, when all the Board Members had made their selection after praying, it was unanimous. One hundred percent of

300

the votes were for Sue. Only then did I tell the Board that the other candidate had withdrawn herself from consideration. Unknowingly, they had each selected the only candidate still in the running. For me, the important thing about that "test" was that I knew I could trust the Board of Directors to pray about an important matter and arrive at the right decision.

As it turned out, Sue has been the most incredible HR Director that ever worked with me. Because we try to promote from within, and many of our ex-addict graduates have many issues, it has been imperative that Sue have an extraordinary amount of patience and wisdom. In addition, as the Director of Human Resources, her discernment has definitely been a true asset to Faith Farm.

It has been so comforting for me to know that I can trust the Board of Directors with proper direction when they say they will pray about a matter before making an important decision. This was extraordinary confirmation for me.

# VIDEO

*"For your Father knoweth what things
ye have need of, before ye ask him."* Matthew 6:8

I was really up tight. I had two days to go before the $15,000 was due on the video I had done about Faith Farm Ministries. I felt in my heart that a video was a necessity for the most extraordinary ministry I had ever seen. Faith Farm is a free, 9-month, drug and alcohol, addiction recovery program that supports itself through its social micro-enterprise, such as cattle, orange groves, recycling, auto auctions, and thrift stores. However, as the new Executive Director, I had exceeded my limit of expenditures without Board of Director approval. I felt my job might be in jeopardy. The video cost $28,000, and I had received the donation of the "soft costs" of scripting, scheduling, and narration. However, the camera, video and editing time were "hard costs" that could not be donated, and they remained due. I wanted the video to be of highest quality, in High Definition. We hired the cable people, who do the spectacular "Animal Planet" videos, to do the filming. I had 90-days to pay for it, but the $15,000 balance was now due in two days with no more extensions allowed. I prayed every day for the extra funds to arrive miraculously, but I was down to two days. I was getting nervous. I really stuck my neck out this time.

You might ask why I would jeopardize my new job by going out on a limb like this. When I came to South Florida, I would ask everyone I met who had heard of Faith Farm, "Do you know what Faith Farm does?" "Oh sure" they would answer, "They're a Thrift Store." I would then ask, "Do you know what they do with the money from the Thrift Store?" They would always answer, "No," or "I'm not sure." Therefore, I believed we needed to get the story

303

out. We needed to tell people what wonderful, life-changing work went on behind the thrift store enterprise. We needed to tell people about the good cause that benefited from the money. It was 9-minutes of student testimonies about their changed lives. To this day, I cannot watch the video without tears, and I have seen it numerous times. The video is a great tool telling about the dramatic life change that occurs at Faith Farm. It depicts the transformation of former addicts and alcoholics into productive, positive citizens. It shows that restoration is possible by bringing men and women home to their spouses, transformed by God.

However, in spite of the great results the informational video produced within the community, the changed lives it depicted, and my daily prayers, I still faced a deadline in two days, and we still had not received the extra $15,000 needed. I knew the project was important. I believed that it was necessary for the ministry, and I had prayed earnestly for the money. However, my time was up.

Two days before the payment was due, I was opening my stack of mail. I noticed an envelope with a return address for a law firm in Miami. Fearing some kind of legal action, I opened it first. It was a letter from an attorney in Miami. She was working on settlement of an estate for a woman who passed away almost two years prior. She said I would find an enclosed check for $15,000 that her deceased client had willed to Faith Farm from her estate. Hallelujah! We can pay the $15,000 invoice … and on time! Prayer does work! Patience might be required while waiting for the answer, but sometimes, He has already answered the prayers, and the money is on its way. We just do not know it yet.

The most interesting thing to me about this extraordinary answer to prayer is that scripture says in Matthew 6:8, *"Our Father*

304

*knows what things we have a need for, even before we ask Him."* True. Two years prior to beginning to pray for this money, the bequest was made to Faith Farm without our knowledge. Moreover, the bequest was the exact amount of $15,000 needed for what I had been praying, and it paid exactly on time! This was a tremendous faith-builder for me. I KNOW the Bible is true, but it is especially gratifying when one gets to experience it in current time, in real life situations, and in answers to prayers of faith. When you are praying for a need in your life, it is always good to remember and lean upon Matthew 6:8, which says, *"... for your Father knoweth what things ye have need of, before ye ask Him."*

This was an extraordinary event in my life ... a timely, pre-ordained, answer to prayer.

On July 25, 2014, Dean O. Webb presided at the Ribbon Cutting Ceremony
For the new "BRIDGE OF HOPE" ... DEDICATED TO THE THOUSANDS WHO CROSS THIS
BRIDGE TO A TRANSFORMED LIFE ... RESTORING HOPE ... ONE LIFE AT A TIME!

# CONDEMNED BRIDGE

*"For your Father knoweth what things ye have need of,
before ye ask Him."* Matthew 6:8

The bridge onto the Faith Farm Ministries' Boynton Beach Campus in Palm Beach County, Florida, was condemned. Authorities said that not even an automobile could cross it. This was a critical situation because it is the only ingress and egress for the 90-acre site of the recovery ministry. Surrounded by canals, the ministry support comes from income generated by an onsite thrift store. There are hundreds of automobiles crossing the bridge daily. In addition, semi tractor-trailers deliver food, furniture, and donated items to support the ministry operations. Without the bridge access, we are essentially closed. In fact, we are marooned and isolated by a moat of water-filled canals. All cash flow from the micro-business enterprises will cease and the ministry will have no money to operate.

Earlier, the Campus Director, Troy, had noticed some erosion. They kept filling the void with asphalt. After many repeated, "fixes" that kept sinking, we called an engineer. They sent divers into the canal, and they x-rayed the 50-year old bridge. They verified severe erosion beneath the concrete side supports, and they were obligated to report it to the Lake Worth Drainage District (LWDD), which was the controlling entity in that area with oversight of the canals. When LWDD got the reports, they had no choice but to condemn the bridge.

Upon appeal, they said if we put in crutch bents (steel I-beams supported by pile-driven posts) under the bridge to support it, we could drive automobiles across, but still no semi tractor-trailer trucks. They gave us one year to complete a new bridge under those conditions. The crutch bents would cost almost $180,000 and the bridge would cost almost an additional million dollars. WOW! We never saw this coming.

We put in the crutch bents within the month. Then, upon approval of the work, we began our year to design, permit and request bids for replacement with a new bridge. Meanwhile, semi-trucks loaded with food, furniture and other deliveries, had to park on the grassy shoulder alongside U.S. Highway 441 next to our entrance, while we backed up our smaller box-trucks and loaded them from the semi-trucks. Multiple trips across the crutch-bent-supported bridge were necessary to unload and handle everything coming into the ministry multiple times.

Banks bombarded us with offers wanting to make us a loan. I had to tell them that we never borrow money. For over 62 years, this ministry had lived by the verse in Romans 13:8, which states, *"Owe no man anything, but to love one another...."* We simply did not have debt or owe anything.

We put the bridge construction design out for bid. Four companies bid on the project. Since our bridge designer said all four were qualified, we selected the lowest bid. When notified of their selection, the President of the company asked for our financials. Upon receiving them, the President called me and said, "You don't have any money." I said, "I know that. You did not ask me if we had any money. You asked me to send you our financials." He then asked, "How are you going to pay us? Who is your lender?"

At that point, I informed him that in history spanning over six decades, we have had a policy of not borrowing money, and we were not going to start now. I said, "God has always provided for us

308

and we will pray for Him to do it now also. This is His ministry, not ours." He said he would have to think about this. A week later, he called back and said, "I don't know why I'm doing this, but I'll start construction and permitting." I told him, "We will be praying."

Meanwhile, how do we get over a million dollars for this unexpected bridge crisis? We all began to pray. We sent out email blasts to customers about the need. A reporter saw our "condemned bridge" sign erected on the highway and did a TV story on the local news regarding the urgent need. A newspaper reporter called and said, "For some reason, I took a different way to work today, and I saw your sign. I smell a story here!" She came out with a photographer and did a second section, front-page article with a half-page color picture of the bridge. Some people responded with checks, cash, and donations on our web site. A nearby mall restaurant gave 20% of their checks on Tuesdays and Thursdays to the "Save the Bridge" campaign. A small foundation sent a $5,000 check after seeing the news. Ten weeks later, we were up to only $90,000 of the 1.14 million we needed. We had never developed a donor base for gifts. All support came in the form of calls requesting a free pickup of donated household items to our thrift store for resale, which funds the ministry. We even received donated autos, which we sold at our annual auction. Typically, however, we did not receive cash support. How were we ever going to get over a million dollars donated?

I remember one week when we received a $93,000 draw request on the bridge and could not pay it. We did the only thing we knew to do ... We prayed. The next week, we received a letter from an attorney who said her client did a *fifth* codicil to his will on April 30th and passed away 90-days later on July 30th." She provided a check for $100,000 to Faith Farm, which represented the change he had put in his will. We met the last bridge draw. Just as Matthew 6:8 states, "... *for your Father knoweth what things ye have need of, before ye ask Him."*

My sister in California is in her 80s and living on social security ... she sent in $500. My nephew visited, saw the need, and donated $500. I was doing a radio show and mentioned the bridge crisis. While on the air, Anita, the host, searched her purse and found $100 cash, which she handed to me while "On-the-Air" during the radio program. The Bridge designer even contributed. God supplied the funds from every possible source, and we finally held the Grand Opening Ribbon Cutting event. It took everything we had or could scrape together, but it worked. God provided the entire amount needed, and in time. We were never late on a draw request.

We wondered why in the world God would let this bridge be condemned. We wondered why He would have us go to such horrendous expense to upgrade the bridge. We soon got the answer. Officials announced that a local homebuilder would be building over 5,200 new homes within a 2-mile radius of our Thrift store. Auto traffic was going to increase dramatically in the future. Although bad at the time, the new bridge was for our eventual good. We would have never wished this crisis on anyone, including ourselves. However, this extraordinary event positioned Faith Farm to accommodate future growth and customers, in advance of the need to fund the ministry. The Thrift Store on this property generates 60% of our entire ministry's cash flow. God really does know what things ye have need of, even before you ask Him. God is good, all the time.

# CABIN FLOOD

*"According to your faith be it unto you."* Matthew 9:29

My favorite place was destroyed. The Yellow River near Stone Mountain, Georgia, rose 19 feet. Water levels rose up to the kitchen cabinets in the 145-year-old log cabin by the river in Atlanta. The raging river washed up under the deck and lifted it up to a spiked point in the sky. The bottom three logs were torn out of place; each one 18 ft. long on the river's side. The raging river washed freely into the old log cabin. A 26" TV console cabinet washed from the living room down the hallway until it could not get through a door and came to rest against a door jam. Mud was deep in the floor after water rose four feet up the walls before receding. Everything from the floor up to 48" high was destroyed. The government recorded it as a "500 Year Flood Event." Over $200,000 in antiques were ruined. The biggest fear was mold.

The Yellow River flooded the cabin when it rose 19' and left a 4' high trail of water and mud damage throughout.

Dr. Andy Steinhauser, one of my son-in-laws, took a week off work and began to tear out everything four feet and lower ... floors, sheetrock, wooden planked walls, ductwork, cabinets ... everything. My other son-in-law, Michael Williams, used his contacts to get commercial dehumidifiers shipped in from South

311

Carolina. No dehumidifiers were available in Georgia due to the extensive rains and flooding statewide. Because it was a 500-year flooding event, everything was in short supply and unavailable. It took a week to gut the cabin and get everything in huge dumpsters. They sealed the cabin with plastic tarps taped shut to let the dehumidifiers try to dry out everything that remained. I was devastated. I had no insurance, and this is where I intended to retire. Because the cabin was so close to the river, 12-15 feet, and in a flood plain, I had been unable to get flood insurance. I had tried to purchase insurance since I purchased the cabin in 1981. What was I going to do? We had no hope except prayer.

The government instructed FEMA (Federal Emergency Management Agency) to look at destroyed homes in the flood plain. When I contacted them, they said it could not be a second home. Only primary residences could get assistance from FEMA. Their criteria for a primary residence was that you had to live in it more than 50% of the time, or a minimum of 6 months plus a day, every year. Because I had gone from 100% occupancy to only trips back to Atlanta to see children and grandchildren since taking my job in South Florida, I could not qualify. However, they said they had to send an agent out there anyway, since I had applied. I scraped together every photograph not destroyed by the flood to show the agent when he came out. I could show him pictures of a showplace full of antiques and paintings, to verify it was not just a vacation, second home. I showed him that this is where I lived before I took the Florida job, and where I intended to return to retire. He took dimensions and scaled out a floor plan. Since I had no insurance, I was unable to do anything about this restoration unless FEMA helped. I could not even sell the old place for scrap, in its current condition. We prayed, but the agent left without saying a word.

We prayed and prayed that God would somehow help us. Unless we could restore the cabin, it had no value, and we had no money to do it ourselves. We returned to Florida and back to my job. We heard nothing from the FEMA agent's visit.

About three weeks later in Florida, I was on my laptop at home, logging on to pay some bills online. When I got to my bank page, I began to cry. I yelled to my wife Cindy to come quick ... to look. She thought something was wrong because I was sobbing so hard. I could only point to the bank entry on my computer that said:

"FEMA - Deposit: $30,000"

I could not believe it. The Agent must have acknowledged that this was really our "permanent home," and we were entitled to some help. With that seed money, we were able to start renovations, which took a year and a half. The FEMA money gave us a head start on the $100,000, the eventual cost to restore the cabin completely, including new logs, appliances, cooling and heating. The code inspectors required us to replace all plumbing and wiring from four-feet down. We ripped up and threw away everything that was wet and soaked in water, including the destroyed hardwood flooring. Dehumidifiers successfully removed all moisture so we have not been subject to mold. The FEMA miracle was the difference between a 145-year-old rotten shell of logs worth nothing, and a fully restored log cabin that is not only livable, but also very hospitable and inviting. Ironically, since the cabin's destruction by the by flood, the government ordered me to get "flood insurance," which I had been trying to get for over 30 years. WOW! What a turnaround ... from "not allowed" to "mandated." This extraordinary event allowed a 100% construction update, plus the flood insurance coverage. The cabin and its contents now have FLOOD insurance.

I also registered the cabin with the Government of Georgia for a possible movie site location, and I will receive payment if chosen. What a reversal. Is not God an awesome God?

Our beautiful 147-year-old log cabin in Stone Mountain, Georgia, is located on the Yellow River. The cabin was completely refurbished after the flood.

# DAUGHTERS

*"Children are a heritage of the Lord."* Psalms 127:3

I have two daughters, Catherine and Christine. They are perfect. They have never been anything but a blessing to me. Because of my job, I am privy to stories of children on drugs, alcohol addiction, illegal and pharmaceutical addiction. I know how they put their families through "hell." I am blessed that I cannot relate to those stories. My daughters have always been a blessing and a total benefit to our family. I do not know why I am so blessed with this experience of wonderful bliss with them. I know I do not deserve it. I was ornery when I was growing up, so I am reaping benefits I did not sow.

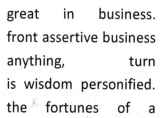

They both are great in business. Catherine is the out-front assertive business woman, who can sell anything, turn companies around, and is wisdom personified. She can turn around the fortunes of a company, while she manages a 2-year old at home. She has a close walk with the Lord, and she is passionate about spiritual things. Catherine is a wordsmith. She is the one I turned to when I needed a catchy title for this book.

Christine has always had an equestrian business at home. She has an eye for horses. She breeds horses and teaches equestrian, hunter-jumper students in her back yard. She runs an equestrian barn and business and provides lessons in the riding ring behind her home, while she manages four boys, with all their energy and after-school activities.

I have been able to accomplish so much more in my life because I have children, who are so loving, so self-sufficient, and so accomplished at so many things. I have no "drag" on my finances, time, efforts, or emotions that are negative. I only have positive reinforcement when I interface with my children. I have thanked God every day for blessing me with such wonderful daughters that are self-sufficient, driven, and motivated to do the right thing. Not only that, but they both married the most wonderful men; Michael in finances and accounting; and, Dr. Steinhauser in education.

"God, I thank You for Cathy and Christy in my life. They are extraordinary in their own right." In my case, scripture is truly correct ... "Children are a heritage of the Lord." They have brought nothing but joy into my life. Had I known how all of this would have turned out, I should have definitely had more children.

No matter how successful they are as wives, mothers, and business women, they'll always be "my little girls" to me."

# CYNTHIA MILLER WEBB

*"... with all humility and gentleness, with patience, showing forbearance to one another in love, being diligent to preserve the unity of the Spirit in the bond of peace."* Ephesians 4:2-3 (NAS)

Cynthia Miller Webb ... my wife, "Cindy" ... is an extraordinary woman. She is one of the most loving people I know. She never breaks ties with anyone. I do not communicate with any of my high school or college friends. However, Cindy ... she is still in contact with her "old" friends, and even stays in touch with her students when she was a teacher, counselor, and department chairperson in the public school system in Illinois.

In fact, a couple of Cindy's former students from the second grade came to our wedding reception in Chicago. When I had a chance to sit with one of them, she told me that as a child with "brown skin", she felt out of place. Her teacher, Cindy, had always encouraged her and valued her completely. She told me she was now married with children. She had her doctorate degree and was a clinical psychologist and associate professor. She mentioned how Cindy had made a lasting impact on her life. In fact, this former student recently authored a self-help book. In the acknowledgments, she wrote, "Thanks to every woman who has been a role model in my life, including my second grade teacher, Cynthia Miller Webb, who understood the importance of seeing the potential in every child." That is typical of the enduring relationships Cindy makes with everyone.

When our cabin flooded, Cindy was there to encourage me to hang on when I was hopeless and without resources to rebuild. Unable to get flood insurance because we were so close to the water and being uninsured, I was so hopeless that I was exploring ways to sell the cabin for "scrap" at a discount. I could see no way out! Knowing how much the cabin meant to me, Cindy would not give up. She worked along side me and eventually FEMA bailed us out with a grant that enabled us to rebuild.

Cindy goes to Chicago throughout the year to see her mother and her family and to work in her hometown. While she is there, she meets with her long time friends. While I do not relish her being gone from me, I do take solace in the fact that I know Cindy is in her element, and she is keeping those special connections that she does so well. That is who Cindy is.

Cindy often puts my needs before her own. She unconditionally supports my endeavors to minister at Faith Farm as well as to write books. This is even with the knowledge that she is writing her own children's book, and she puts that on hold to defer to my work and projects.

When we needed to move out of our rental because the owner was selling, Cindy did all the packing up while maintaining the house to "show." She even showed the house and extolled the virtues of the home to a prospective buyer when the realtor did not show up, even though it was not to our benefit for them to like the house because we didn't want to move.

When we had gone months looking at rental homes and could not find one that was suitable or was not already rented before we could get there, Cindy made up a "vision board." She went to a craft store and purchased a tri-fold presentation board. She cut out pictures and words from magazines of what we wanted in a rental and glued them all over the board. She then had us review the board and criteria we wanted in a rental home. We laid hands on the board daily and prayed for God to bring us a rental home with the criteria we desired.

Cindy has really conquered a tough roll … that of being a "grandmother" in the position held by my daughter's birth mother, Bertie, who passed away. When the grandkids came along, they have only known Cindy in that role. Cindy has totally endeared herself to the

318

grandchildren of both daughters. She loves them; and they know it and love her back. She remembers their birthdays and special events, and she is a total support to them. I cannot imagine a more loving grandmother than Cindy.

Cindy is an extraordinary support to me. I could not do my job as Executive Director at Faith Farm Ministries without Cindy's total support. Cindy's long-term relationships and her willingness to defer her own ambitions and desires are quite fascinating to me. She is the epitome of a true support to me and a kind and loving person. In fact, if she were to pass away, I think I would put on her tombstone: "The Kindest Soul I've Ever Known." That would sum up Cindy's life.

# AIRLINE BARF BAG

*"A man's heart deviseth his way: but the
Lord directeth his steps."* Proverbs 16:9

I was flying back to my job in South Florida. I had been to a wonderful leadership conference that stimulated so many ideas, and I could not wait to write them down. I had a pen, but could find no paper. Therefore, I took a white, paper "barf bag" from the pocket of the airline seat in front of me. It was thick, so I needed no support for the paper. I laid it on my knee and began listing things to do when I arrived home. I did not write long sentences, only a bullet point list of 1-3 words each describing ideas to implement. The ideas flowed like water, and I wrote the list as quickly as my mind could think of them. I wrote them down as they popped into my head, in no particular order of importance. I wrote them small, so I could capture as many ideas as I could possibly think of, and get them on one side. The list of ideas filled the whole length of the bag. I was so proud of myself for capturing dozens of ways for improvement that would make dramatic, good directional changes in operations. I placed the bag in the fold of a magazine I carried on board to read during the flight.

Monday morning, I arrived at work so eager to begin on my list of operational improvements. Immediately, there was a line at my door. The HR Director had a personnel problem she needed to discuss that was so serious it might require termination of an employee's employment. The Controller needed funds transferred immediately to the operations account that was drained to make payroll last Friday. An Intake Counselor had an emergency with a student resident to discuss. The Pastor asked me to speak in church for him the next Sunday, because he was going on vacation. All three farm Directors had urgent situations they had been holding to discuss with me … and, so it continued.

The next day was not much different in intensity, but different problems. By the end of the week, I had completely forgotten about the barf bag. I had not looked at it or even thought about it. The urgent problems that were immediate crowded out the written ideas that were important. Weeks later, I came across the barf bag, still tucked into the magazine I carried in my briefcase. I realized I needed to change my situation to avoid ever losing the traction needed to follow through with implementing ideas … like those I had listed on the barf bag. They were good ideas.

Now, I come in on Saturdays when I have no interruptions. I lay out the implementation for those new ideas, and even send emails to the appropriate staff members with instructions necessary to implement them. I never again want to lose the momentum of extraordinary, innovative ideas for change, by another "Barf bag" experience, where the "immediate and urgent" issues override and crowd out the larger "important" issues.

# THE PAINT'S NOT DRY YET

*".. the Lord will hear when I call unto Him."* Psalms 4:3

We did not want to move. We were happy in our rental home that we had been in for years. However, our landlord wanted us to buy her house, and we only wanted to rent. Although the house was not large, we were in a community that had all the amenities you could want, except golf. They had the largest pool and pool area I have ever seen. There was a restaurant, exercise facilities, indoor pool, sauna and steam room, library, billiard rooms, poker/canasta card rooms … all off the pool area. It was a "5-Star Resort", as my son-in-law said when he visited from Atlanta. It even had a beautiful ballroom that showed free, first-release movies on Friday night. There were too many amenities to get around to using them all.

I rented the home in 2008, in the middle of the 2007-2009 housing bubble burst, so I had rented at a good price. Now that the market was recovering, my landlord wanted to sell. Since I did not want to own another house (I still had my house in Atlanta,) and she started by quoting a steep rent increase, which I met. When she jumped the rent another $700 in mid 2013, we finally said we could not renew the lease and began looking.

Because so many people had been foreclosed out of the upside-down house loans, it seemed that everyone who walked away from their homes were now renters. They could not buy another home because of their ruined credit. As a result, homes for rent were in high demand. We would search for rentals on-line. However, before I could look at an available property after work or on the weekend, homes were already rented. While our landlord was being kind enough to keep extending our lease month to month, she was unhappy. She really wanted to take advantage of the upswing in housing prices, and we were hindering that as renters. She listed the house with a Realtor for sale, and we were under the gun to find a decent place to rent. While we really wanted to be packing up our household goods, we kept our word and kept the place looking nice with all our furnishings in place so the house would show well to prospective buyers ... our concession for the rent extensions.

One of the difficult things in Florida for someone wanting a long-term lease is that you cannot rent through a Realtor on a lease for more than one year. After the renting experience we just had, we decided that we wanted a long-term lease the next go-around. However, that seemed out of the question. We enlisted our own Realtor to help us expand our search, find a rental and screen for a landlord who desired a good, long-term tenant. Although the availability of houses for rent expanded, either we found them under contract by the time we could look at them, or they were unsuitable. We encountered ridiculous situations, from homes with all the walls covered in mirrors, to one whose owner insisted he maintain all of his tools and power equipment in the garage for the upkeep and maintenance on all his other rental property. We would never know when he would be coming over to open the garage door to get equipment to do repairs or handle an emergency.

A foreign entity purchased some of the nicer homes we liked. They bought almost 3,000 homes out of foreclosure in South Florida. Crazy enough, they did not use a Realtor. You had to go on-line and put in all your personal information from bank accounts to social security numbers. There were no security controls over personal information. Our Realtor could not even deal with another Realtor. The on-line posted complaints from those who already rented from this foreign company appeared to be nightmares. They could not get maintenance on their units. They were unresponsive for vital repairs, including destroyed furniture issues due to unfixed leaks. This company now had control of the majority of the houses we liked. They were paying cash and buying up everything directly from the banks doing the foreclosures. We felt trapped.

After extending our current month-to-month lease for 7 months at stair-stepped rent increases, while maintaining the house for presenting to prospective purchasers, we finally called my sister, Ann, in California. She is one of the most spiritual people I know and a real person of prayer. We explained the desperate situation and she said she would pray for our rental situation. Meanwhile, we continued to look.

Earlier, my wife, Cindy, purchased a tall, tri-fold poster board to be our shared "vision board." She cut out magazine pictures and wording of what we wanted in a rental house. She created a collage all over the poster board. We would pray over that board every morning and before bedtime, reminding God of our heart's desires, regardless of the bleak circumstances.

About a month later, my sister, Ann, called me from California. She said, "Dean, I don't know what to make of this, how to interpret it, or what it means, but I feel God telling me that the reason you haven't found a house to rent yet is because 'The Paint's Not Dry Yet.'" I told her that the only thing that meant to me was that "our" house had not yet come onto the market. Our Realtor kept looking.

In less than a month, Cindy called me and said the Realtor had a home for rent that had just come on the market. It was an older home and larger than our requirements. It was more expensive than our target rent, but the owner was a Christian who really preferred a longer-term tenant since he had no intention of selling. I told Cindy to make an appointment immediately to meet with the Realtor and go look at the house.

We loved the neighborhood and the house. The crews were in the house painting and doing minor repairs from the last renter. While looking through the house, I was fascinated by the large pantry in the kitchen. Large 5-gallon paint buckets blocked access. Since the light was off in the pantry and the door was standing open, I placed my right hand on the doorframe to lean into the pantry to look. One of the workers saw me and yelled, "Don't lean on that! The paint's not dry yet." When I pulled my hand away, it had white paint on it with the pattern of the door molding. *This was our house.*

I called my sister that night to share the specific details of her answer to prayer. We were both amazed at how God is so gracious to be our guide to answer our prayers.

At this writing, we have gone through the first year's Realtor rental contract and are now able to extend the lease to a longer term individually, which was the goal of both parties to the Lease. In summary, I do not know how I would be able to function without knowing I could rely on God to give direction and to answer specific prayers. God is so good to be there when we are desperate for Him to intervene in our affairs and when we cry out to Him. For us, this was an extraordinary solution. Thank you, Ann, for praying ...

and, thank you, God, for your direction through prayer. Psalms 4:3 does say, "...*the Lord will hear when I call unto Him.*"

# BOOMER SOONER

Hanging on the wall of my cabin near Stone Mountain, Georgia, just East of Atlanta, is a large, framed deed to 40 acres in Oklahoma. The property was assigned to my Grandfather, John T. Webb, for serving as a Federal Marshall during the Great Land Rush of Oklahoma on April 22, 1889, commissioned by President Benjamin Harrison.

Due to improved ranch and farming techniques, the government decided that the barren land in Indian Territory could be productive farmland. The Federal Government, under President Benjamin Harrison, had decided to offer 1.9 million acres in Indian Territory (now, Oklahoma) to those who would stake a claim and farm and improve the land they claimed. The government allowed people to stake out up to 160 acres. If they farmed it and improved the land, in five years they would receive a deed to the 160 acres, which they would legally own for life. The areas of unassigned, settled lands included parts of the current Cleveland, Kingfisher, Logan and Payne Counties. In the seven weeks prior to the Land Rush date, more than 50,000 hopefuls camped out in tents on the border starting line.

The set-up was this ... Everyone participating in the great Land Rush would line up their horses or horse-drawn wagons on the Indian Territory border. At noon, on April 22, 1889, the cannon at Fort Reno would fire. When the Marshalls heard the "boom," they would signal that they heard the official "boom" all the way down the borderline to each Marshall, one by one. Then the "Boomers" began their dash across the landscape to choose a parcel of 160 acres and stake out a claim for them. Of course, the ones on horseback could make it further inland faster than those pulling wagons. Some settlers took trains, but to be fair, the trains could not go faster than the fastest horseback rider's speed. At some point, railroad passengers would outdistance those on exhausted horses, jump off and stake a claim to land.

Some folks, like my Grandfather, decided to be deputized as a Federal Marshall to keep order and to keep out the "Sooners." For that duty, the Marshalls received a deed of 40 acres, or one-fourth of the total 160 acres they might have staked out if they had participated in the Land Rush. That is the deed hanging on my wall and signed by the President.

The "Sooners" were those who, because of greed, jumped the gun and went in sooner than the April 22 date and tried to stake out a claim early. They violated the "Sooner Clause" of the Indian Appropriation Act, by hiding out in brush and in ravines to be undetected, so they could get a jump on the competition. The Marshalls worked to prevent this from happening, but could not discover, catch, and arrest everyone. Therefore, the Boomer Sooners caused conflicting claims for the same and overlapping land. The courts tied these lands up in litigation for years. In fact, President Theodore Roosevelt did not sign my Grandfather's Deed until April 4, 1904.

By 1907, the Indian Territory combined with the 1.9 million acres of the Land Rush formed the 46th State of the Union ... Oklahoma. Homage to the Land Rush was acknowledged by Oklahoma's adoption of the nickname, "Sooner State." In fact, if you ever watch an OU (University of Oklahoma) football-sporting event, you will instantly hear the band strike up the fight song, "Boomer Sooner" upon scoring a touchdown.

My Grandfather's Deed is a constant reminder of my historical roots in Oklahoma. My birth in Oklahoma is rooted in history, of which my Grandfather played an important part. Not everyone can point back to a family member's dramatic involvement in the history of his or her birth state. Personally, I think that is extraordinary.

Land Rush of 1889 (Wikipedia) My grandfather was deputized as a Federal Marshal to keep the "Sooners" out. In return, he received 40 acres of land in Oklahoma.

Although the land rush occurred in 1889, the actual deed for 40 Acres was issued to my Grandfather, John Webb, on April 4, 1904, and signed by Theodore Roosevelt. The original hangs in my log cabin home in Atlanta.

# EPILOGUE

It was about 9:30 PM on a Wednesday night after attending services at my Father's church. I was knocking on my parent's bedroom door. It was August 15, just four days before my fourth birthday on August 19. My mother opened the door and I said, "I want to ask Jesus to come into my heart." She called to my father, "Oliver, come here!" They knelt on either side of me by their bed and I prayed a simple prayer, asking Jesus to come into my heart.

I know what you are probably thinking. *"A three year old, almost four, doesn't know or understand what they are doing at that age."* I say that because I have heard it before.

I cannot speak about other four year olds … only for myself. I knew what I was doing. I knew the commitment I was making by my decision. I have no doubt that my whole life of relationship to God began at that moment, just before I turned four. I believe my life-long commitment as a child of God is responsible for my experiencing so many answers to prayer and supernatural outcomes in many events in my life. It has been an extraordinary walk with Him.

John 3:16 says, *"For God so loved the world that He gave His only begotten son, that whosoever believeth on Him should not perish, but have everlasting life."*

In John 5:24, Jesus said, *"… He that heareth My Word, and believeth on Him that sent Me, hath everlasting life and shall not come into condemnation: but is passed from death unto life."*

Proverbs 16:9 says, *"A man's heart deviseth his way: but the Lord directeth his steps."*

And, in Psalms 37:23 it says, *"The steps of a good man are ordered by the Lord: and He delighteth in his way."*

I was filled with the "Word of God." We practically *lived* in the church *(my perspective)* while sitting under my father's ministry. I could not escape the process and passion of having to make a decision to follow Him. During my life and its extraordinary happenings, both good and bad, I knew God was in control, and that He had the best intentions for me and my life. I am here to tell you … that brings extraordinary peace … even in the storms of life. Walking with God is an extraordinary experience. This 4 year old made the right choice. Walking in a spiritual walk with God turns your life events from ordinary to extraordinary!

# Another book by Dean O. Webb

100% of your purchase of U-TURN To God goes directly to Faith Farm Ministries' free drug and alcohol addiction recovery program. Read these testimonies of broken lives changed by the power of God.

Available at:
**Amazon.com**
and
**FaithFarm.org**
**$14.95 US**
**ISBN# 978099148-524**

Dean Webb has done an excellent job of bringing a book to the reader that testifies of the grace, mercy, and goodness of the Lord, as He stands waiting, with open arms, to welcome home His prodigal sons and daughters, whose lives have been shattered by addiction. This book is a celebration of all who have passed through the gates of Faith Farm Ministries and were set free by the power of Almighty God.

No one who made a choice to become an addict. Addiction is destructive for families and communities. An old Japanese proverb says, "First the man takes a drink, then the drink takes a drink, then the drink takes the man." Webster's New World Dictionary defines rehabilitation as, "to restore to rank, reputation, etc., which one has lost; to put back in good condition." Faith Farm Ministries is NOT committed to putting "back in good condition." We are committed to regeneration. Webster's defines regeneration as, "spiritually reborn; renewed; to cause to be spiritually reborn; to be made anew."

No one can argue that addiction is now at epidemic levels. Everyone knows someone; a loved one, a neighbor, a co-worker or friend who has addiction issues. Overcoming codependency can be as difficult a challenge as overcoming an addiction.

Faith Farm lives out its purpose for our students daily: "Restoring Hope... One Life at a Time" and these are their stories. Please enjoy reading them.

Made in the USA
San Bernardino, CA
17 February 2017